THE UNITED STATES
IN WORLD AFFAIRS

**FOUNDATIONS OF AMERICAN GOVERNMENT
AND POLITICAL SCIENCE**

Joseph P. Harris, Consulting Editor

Revisions and additions have been made to keep this series up to date and to enlarge its scope, but its purpose remains the same as it was on first publication: To provide a group of relatively short treatises dealing with major aspects of government in modern society. Each volume introduces the reader to a major field of political science through a discussion of important issues, problems, processes, and forces and includes at the same time an account of American political institutions. The author of each work is a distinguished scholar who specializes in and teaches the subjects covered. Together the volumes are well adapted to serving the needs of introductory courses in American government and political science.

ANDREW HACKER   The Study of Politics: The Western Tradition and American Origins, 2d ed.

C. HERMAN PRITCHETT   The American Constitutional System, 3d ed.

HUGH A. BONE and AUSTIN RANNEY   Politics and Voters, 3d ed.

ROWLAND EGGER   The President of the United States, 2d ed.

JOSEPH P. HARRIS   Congress and the Legislative Process, 2d ed.

JOHN J. CORSON and JOSEPH P. HARRIS   Public Administration in Modern Society

CHARLES O. LERCHE, JR.   America in World Affairs, 2d ed.

CHARLES R. ADRIAN   Governing Our Fifty States and Their Communities, 3d ed.

H. FRANK WAY, JR.   Liberty in the Balance: Current Issues in Civil Liberties, 3d ed.

PAUL SEABURY   The United States in World Affairs

THE UNITED STATES
IN WORLD AFFAIRS

PAUL SEABURY
PROFESSOR OF POLITICAL SCIENCE
UNIVERSITY OF CALIFORNIA, BERKELEY

McGRAW-HILL BOOK COMPANY
New York   San Francisco   St. Louis   Düsseldorf   Johannesburg
Kuala Lumpur   London   Mexico   Montreal   New Delhi   Panama
Rio de Janeiro   Singapore   Sydney   Toronto

This book was set in Helvetica by Rocappi, Inc. The editors were Robert P. Rainier and Ronald Q. Lewton, the designer was Janet Bollow and the production supervisor was Michael A. Ungersma.

The printer and binder was The Book Press Company.

THE UNITED STATES IN WORLD AFFAIRS

Printed in the United States of America.

Library of Congress Cataloging in Publication Data

Seabury, Paul.
  The United States in world affairs.

  (Foundations of American government and political science)
  1. United States—Foreign relations. I. Title. II. Series.
JX1407.S38   327.73   72-4817
ISBN 0-07-055895-7
ISBN 0-07-055894-9 (pbk.)

1234567890 BPBP 79876543

PREFACE

This introduction to United States foreign policy appears at a time when a quarter of a century of conventional assumptions about America's role in world politics are being widely challenged and altered. Many recent books that introduce students to this area of politics tend to describe in detail the current posture of the nation in many regions and in many functional problems of the world society. But the current state of uncertainty on so many scores is such that I have chosen, instead, to take a different course. Foreign policy is principally a matter of choosing and acting. This book singles out what I regard as central elements that affect policy judgments and that lead to decisions, choices, and action.

Albert Sorel somewhere referred to "an eternal dispute between those who imagine the world to suit their policies, and those who correct their policy to suit the world." Whichever camp one belongs to, it remains the case that the world of policy is a time-continuum in which judgment and action both are directed, not at past achievements, faults, and errors, but to current exigencies and future goals and contingencies. In this, the deterrence of bad futures must rank equally as high as the aspiration to attain good ones.

PAUL SEABURY

CONTENTS

1 GENERAL THEORY AND HISTORICAL REALITIES

That the United States currently is the most influential nation among nations, some welcome, many regret, but few would dispute. Its land and people are but a small fraction of the total geographic surface and population of the world. Yet for more than half a century, its influence on international affairs has been extraordinary and it continues to be so. This may seem less strange, when we consider that most of these influences have not been part of any grand national design but rather have arisen as aggregate effects and by-products of an extraordinarily dynamic culture. In a world system today whose distinctive features, historically new, arise from applications of technology to human affairs, America in the twentieth century has been at the forefront of such innovations. In the unleashing of new sources of natural energy, America has reached a stage at which nearly one-half of the world's total energy production is annually consumed by her own population—6 percent of the total population of the world. That the quality of American life leaves much to be desired, few would dispute. Yet the influences of this affluent, open society upon its environment are great and undiminished.

This tapping of new sources of power and their focused orchestration into new systems of use have had ambiguous consequences. All forms of power are ambivalent, subject to both use and abuse; so that while it may be said that for most human beings historically, and for most who now are alive, the grief of life lies in constraints of poverty and impotence, this nearly universal truism by and large is not true for Americans. For them, the paradoxes of power, not of impotence, are the source of current discontents. As new forms of power (and the new options of action they bring) multiply, so too do the questions of their management and control assume great dimensions. To cite one mundane example: The high incidence of crimes of theft in America are not unrelated to the ease of an affluent enlightened society in both producing and replacing goods; an unnamed auto theft ringleader in New York recently justified his profession on grounds that everyone gained: the victim, by insurance compensation, could gain a new car; the purchaser of the stolen goods buys one more cheaply than on the open market; the producer, by the stimulus this mechanism of transfer affords, expands his operations; and innumerable jobs are provided for insurance agents. Such a view would be inconceivable in a "backward" society.[1]

This situation is also apparent in the realm of war weaponry; in this, the acquisition of new forms of material force poses ever-new questions about the appropriateness of their use in concrete circumstances. Less advanced societies or political systems, may, in their use of blunter and cruder weaponry for political purposes, feel less troubled about such matters since their tools are traditional and thus undramatic; yet for us the proliferation of newly contrived equipment constantly raises in an open society like America new moral questions concerning the proportionality of force to concrete circumstances of human conflict. In the Vietnam War, while much was made of the horrors of air bombing and

[1] Peter Hellman, "Stealing Cars Is a Growth Industry," *New York Times Magazine,* June 20, 1971, pp. 7,41ff.

helicopter raids, less was said of the more intimate and traditional modes employed by an enemy poorly endowed with modern equipment.

This conspicuous posture of the United States in the world arena has often contributed to an analytic confusion between national influence and national purpose in world affairs. If we recall the original meaning of the term "influence," it was an ethereal fluid thought by the ancients to flow from stars and to affect men's actions; such influence (like that of America) might not be contrived and purposeful. Quite the contrary: the national actions of open societies are often random or unintended, both in their origins and their effects. (The collapse of the American economy in the early 1930s was no national policy of the United States, but it drastically influenced the world economy. More commendable internal events in America, unintended and even spontaneous, also have worked their influences upon the surrounding world.)

So too, in the instance of this large and influential nation, the purposeful withholding of strength in international affairs can cause combinations of nations to tilt, as effectively as if American strength had been directly exerted. As George Kennan once said, America is a giant in a small room—whatever move it makes, for whatever purpose, affects all the others. As Americans discovered in the 1930s, to their later dismay, a deliberate American policy of withholding influence from European affairs greatly affected the calculations of European statecraft and fueled the ambitions of Adolf Hitler. As that instance of withholding force in the name of noninvolvement indicates, a policy of nonaction as much influences events as would a policy of action.

The conspicuous position of the United States in a world of nations and its enormous potential for purposive action give rise to distorted conceptions of American power. The presence of great resources in a great nation does not in and of itself indicate their readiness or applicability to purposes of foreign policy at any given time. In point of fact, the vast output of the nation primarily is oriented to the consumer. An authoritarian political system might allocate resources quite differently. If the United States devoted the same proportion of its gross national product (GNP) to national defense as does the Soviet Union, its defense budget would be more than six times its current size.

So also, national will affects the nature of national power. For when foreign policy aims pursued by its government are erratic or feeble, or are widely questioned or objected to by important parts of the public, their credibility and effectiveness are to that extent lessened.

AMERICA IN A WORLD OF TERRITORIAL STATES

A book about theories of American foreign policy must deal first with those features of international politics commonly faced by each sovereign state in the society of nations, regardless of its unique characteristics. These features of the international system derive from the system's distinctive quality; namely, its division into autonomous territorial states, each laying claim to sovereignty over some part of the earth's land, air, waters, and peoples. Within such space, this claim of sovereign authority is absolute. The state recognizes no superior positive law (other than that which may arise from treaty obligations acquiesced to). It recognizes no domestic effect of laws of "foreign" states domestically (other than that accepted through treaty). This claim to sovereignty frequently may be challenged by others (as, in the instance of Arab states' denial of sovereign authority to the state of Israel); the claim of sovereignty may be mocked by real limitations on the effective exercise of authority by the state over this space (as with China during the first half of the twentieth century); also, as in the instance of America's assertion of plenary sovereignty with respect to other states, this assertion is domestically constrained by a constitutional doctrine that limits the exercise of such sovereignty domestically (as does the Bill of Rights of the American Constitution). Conversely, a doctrine of limited federal sovereignty does not apply internationally: the United States government, in its transactions with other states, asserts plenary sovereign rights derived, not from the American Constitution, but from the law of nations.[2]

This decentralized system of sovereign states long has been accepted as the dominant form of political organization in what we call the Western world; recently, as non-Western nations have asserted and gained their independence, the system has gained nearly universal acceptance. But this system is historically contingent; other forms of political organization, including feudalism and empire, have existed; even today, many men reject or deny its validity or see grave defects in

[2] See *United States v. Curtiss-Wright Corp.*, 290 U.S. 304 (1936).

it. In the so-called Western world (the territories of which roughly approximate those of the ancient Roman world), empire preceded the territorial state system, its imperial authority covering most of the land now claimed by the sovereign states of Europe. But this idea of empire—namely, that of a polity coextensive with civilization—is antithetic to the idea of a system of sovereign states. So also, the traditional Chinese view of their place in the world contrasts strikingly with Western views of international politics. Western views of international law stress the sovereignty of equal states (equal in rights if not in capabilities), a doctrine unknown in traditional China, where, classically, the world of political relationships centered about a central Chinese polity; foreign states were regarded as inferior tributaries. Western conceptions of the state system affirm its decentralized character; traditional Chinese views saw it as essentially centered upon one locus of political authority.[3]

THE TWO REALMS
OF AMERICAN POLITICS

For every state, in this decentralized system of states, there are two realms of politics, one domestic and the other external. The first realm entails the internal reconciliation of demands, aspirations, and interests of its own people as these relate to each other; the statecraft of domestic politics entails the adjustment of competing claims within an acknowledged system of laws. In certain states, notably totalitarian ones, the domestic political system is one of forced coordination in which overt political opposition is routinely suppressed and competing ideas of politics are severely punished. In every instance, however, the priorities of politics look inward; typically, they are focused upon satisfying or mollifying interests and aspirations. In industrial societies, for instance, the general welfare now is said to comprise maintenance of full employment, high levels of productivity, fair access to social services, protection of civil rights of citizens, equal access to education, and so forth. Whatever the salient issues of domestic contention may be (and they vary greatly from time to time) their internal reconciliation normally takes the form of new law or revision of old law; known constitutional

---

[3] See C. P. Fitzgerald, *The Chinese View of Their Place in the World*, Oxford University Press, New York, 1964.

procedures constitute the framework in which changes occur. The constitutional norm of "government of laws, not men" signifies the supremacy of law and prohibits the caprice of arbitrary will. Even in most Communist countries today, in practice, there is a growing respect for this constitutional norm—known, in the Soviet Union, as "Socialist legality." By whatever name, we see in this domestic realm the existence of ultimate, sovereign authority, with known or knowable rules and procedures.

The political realm of foreign affairs, however, presents quite a different picture. In this, the nation exists among nations; its own sovereign determinations cannot control or adjudicate its own relations with the others. Its own legislative processes alone cannot make law or reconcile disputes that the nation or its people may have with others. Moreover, the international realm, the environment within which the state exists, is itself a sphere in which major problems arise with which the nation's statecraft must deal continuously and flexibly, without hoping for the kinds of "final solutions" that the domestic legislative process often promises. Here fate often enters, frustrating the aspirations and wishes of domestically oriented politicians. For example, the American Constitution gives the United States Congress the exclusive power to declare war. But as the Supreme Court once noted, war nevertheless can spring "forth suddenly from the parent brain, a Minerva in the full panoply of war"—giving legislators no opportunity to declare it or by law to change the fact of it.[4] American neutrality laws passed by Congress in the mid-1930s sought by unilateral legislative fiat to reduce the possibilities of American involvement in European war; yet these laws, while imposing constraints on behavior of American citizens and government in time of such foreign war, could in no way impose constraints upon the behavior of other states that generated this war, and they proved ultimately a feeble reed upon which American neutrality could lean.

What is often true of war is also true of many other occurrences in the international system; these have a way of altering its general or special configurations, in defiance of the wills and intentions of domestic political leaders or the hopes of public opinion. This indeterminacy of international politics and the possibilities present in it for disadvanta-

---

[4] The Prize Cases, 2B1. 635, 668 (1863).

geous, dangerous, and often rapid changes, contrast sharply with the domestic realm of politics. The character of this international system, diffuse and far more complex than the domestic one, and the high order of risks entailed in purposive action within it, makes the arena of foreign policy one in which—as Chief Justice John Marshall of the United States Supreme Court once said—qualities of "secrecy and despatch" (read: "confidentiality and speed") often are essential for national action, even though in purely domestic affairs such modes of governmental behavior in many instances would be regarded as arbitrary, capricious, and even unconstitutional.

The hazards in this international realm for individual states most often arise from conflicts of interests and aspirations of nations, and no interest may be said to rank higher, for any state, than the concern for the safety of its own political and territorial integrity. This matter of integrity often is referred to as "vital interests" or, in the special language used by America and the Soviet Union in their dealing with each other, as "state interests."[5] Such high-sounding, ambiguous phrases lack specificity, yet they have many grave connotations in practice; their invocation, especially in times of international crisis, connotes invariably a determination to use force to defend them and, of course, entails the possibility of war. Statesmen are obliged to place such matters at the highest level of importance even though, at any given moment, most people may take them for granted.

Quite often, of course, when statesmen invoke "vital interests," the specific matter of contention at hand may, to some, appear arbitrary or capriciously chosen. This is so since important psychological elements are entailed in making the judgment. In the Cuban missile crisis of 1962, President John F. Kennedy invoked American state interests when the Soviet government surreptitiously commenced installation of missile bases in Cuba, designed for nuclear weapons aimed at the American mainland. Some argued then, and some still argue that these installations were less grave a military threat than the Kennedy administration judged them to be; yet for our purposes here, it is important to note that responsible statesmen so judged them at the time and because of their diagnosis took speedy countermeasures, at some grave risk, to compel

[5] Privately to signal to the other that its state interests are entailed in some matter of disputation is to signal that grave issues are involved.

Soviet withdrawal. The place that an event is judged to occupy, in a stream of occurrences, gives it its significance; thus it is that specific matters of grave international disputation often appear in tranquil retrospect to be either trifles or certainly of less weight than the significances that men attached to them at the time.

In this respect, we should notice that states often come to regard their vital (or state) interests as being imperiled even when there may be no clear current intention on the part of an adversary state to seriously abridge or endanger them. This is an extremely troublesome aspect of international politics, for it is often true that a suspicious state may pay more attention to what another *can* do to it of a dangerous nature, than to what that other actually intends, at a given moment, to do; this tendency results in a cautious attention to an adversary's capabilities, rather than simply to its current intentions. This attention to capabilities, it might be added, is not unwarranted, since intentions can change more rapidly than can capabilities. What a nation resolves today to do, or not to do, is not a necessary indicator of its future behavior. At each stage in the course of his European aggrandizement, Hitler repeatedly assured Germany's neighbors that he had "no further territorial ambitions"; perhaps at each moment he may not have had such intentions, but the denied ambitions soon manifested themselves as being within the scope of Germany's capabilities.[6]

NATIONAL INTEGRITY AND NATIONAL SELF-DETERMINATION

The "political and territorial integrity of states," vague and abstract, becomes concrete in historical circumstances. Abridgments of territorial integrity take specific form: the loss of some province or region, the

[6] In 1950, Chinese Communists intervened in the Korean War, doubtless fearing the grave security consequences to their nation if American military power installed itself on the Manchurian border or even moved across that border. From an American vantage point, especially from that of Gen. Douglas MacArthur's command, such apprehensions may have seemed unwarranted, it not being then the intention of United States policy makers to carry the war to China. Yet the apprehensions were nonetheless real, and American policy makers gravely miscalculated—just as, later, Soviet authorities in the Cuban missile crisis misjudged American perceptions.

ripping apart of a once-united polity, the secession of a part or its annexation by some other state. Such specific eventualities endanger the integrity of the whole; the unwished loss of some part of the whole gives rise to the prospect that much more also may be risked. It is in the nature of the occasion in which concrete policy decisions are made, that statesmen must direct themselves, not just to some finite matter at hand, but to future implications entailed in the outcome or disposition of the case. This is especially true of states whose internal cohesiveness is not great; for instance, the Nigerian government's 1968 decision to suppress the Biafran secessionist movement was made, not only to prevent the loss of this important area to the whole Nigerian federation, but also because of a cautious fear that were secession to succeed, the entire federation would fall apart in ruins. Territorial losses may have grave consequences for the general security of the whole. The loss of a region may cripple a nation's geographic security or deprive it of crucial resources: this is especially true when the territorial loss is the gain of some known adversary or when the loss of it symbolically undercuts the cultural rationale of the whole.

Such considerations frequently vie with other principles and values of great political importance. In some instances, a particular political system seems to break asunder by virtue of strongly expressed local desires for self-determination. So, in the early twentieth century, nationalist movements in Central and Eastern Europe, struggling for self-determination within the polyglot Hapsburg empire, threatened the existing stability of the European order and were an important element in provoking the outbreak of World War I in 1914. The final attainment of independence by these nationalities after 1918 was at the expense of the multinational economic order and civic security that the empire had provided. The succession states—small, quarrelsome, and weak—soon became victims of more powerful states far more vicious than the Hapsburgs ever could have been—the Third Reich and Stalin's Russia. Valuable as the abstract principle of national self-determination may seem, especially in an age of mass societies, the price of its fulfillment in many concrete circumstances often is heavy. In Indochina, for instance, millions of lives have been expended by the North Vietnam Communists in two decades of fanatical quest for it. Much more was lost in the instance of Hitler's attempts to bring all Germans "under one roof" of his own new order of things.

Whatever may be said in its favor, the pursuit of national self-determination as end in itself is necessarily oblivious to considerations of international equilibrium and civil tranquility; and it often results in massive conflicts. (This is particularly so in cases where two or more nationality groups contend for supremacy in the same territorial space. The Arab-Israeli conflict, now three decades old, bears witness to this; Arab nationalism contests, not the rights of Zionist self-determination in abstract or the rights of individual Jews to live in Palestine, but "merely" the effective claims of Zionism to politically control territories once predominantly Arab.)

The integrity of states in this spatial sense gives to states authority to regulate transactions and movements across their borders and to manage their own "households." The flow of peoples, goods, and ideas across national boundaries is subject to such regulation. The management of the internal economy lies in the first instance with the state; yet, exaggerated assertion of sovereign authority can strike a hollow note. In practice, nearly all states, except those that are unusually primitive and isolated, depend for their prosperity and their security upon a reasonably congenial surrounding environment. The sufficient conditions for their welfare go beyond the necessary conditions of their sovereign integrity. A zealous affirmation of sovereign rights may transform a state into a self-isolated hermit kingdom; in prohibiting "foreign influences," a state may shut out beneficent as well as malevolent ones. An underdeveloped country that zealously forbids foreign capital investment or nationalizes such investments already made may condemn itself to backwardness. Americans may forget that until 1914 the United States, on balance, was a debtor nation; foreign investments in the United States greatly exceeded American investments abroad. During its crucial developmental years of the nineteenth century, the growth of the American economy was facilitated by its "colonial dependence" on European finance. So also, the openness of America to settlement by foreign migrants and to skills of foreign managers and technicians served as the principal stimulus to its economic growth. A zealous prohibition of entry of foreign influences would have crippled America's growth.

When we speak of this wish for a secure, benign environment, we come across one of the most perplexing aspects of international politics: that "environment" is subjectively perceived by the public and policy makers of each state. In fact (and logically so) each state has its own special foreign environment; each has special, subjectively perceived conceptions of what in that environment best or worst suits its unique interests; and so it is that quite often such interests (each of which possibly may be quite legitimate from a subjective point of view) collide. For instance, immediately after World War II, Stalin contended that the Soviet Union required "friendly states" on its western borders as protection against future resumed attack from that direction; as it worked out in practice, for Eastern European countries, "friendliness" meant subjection to Soviet rule. Exactly the same argument—namely, the need for friendly neighbors—might as well have been made by Poles or Czechs, whose own national independence was crushed to satisfy this Russian craving. The conditions for one state's security may be the conditions of another's insecurity—this, despite protestations to the contrary. To cite a more mundane environmental example, states today embrace various doctrines concerning territorial waters: some claim sovereign authority to a 200-mile limit, while others apply to themselves and others stricter doctrines—the traditional 3-mile limit, for instance. The matter may be cleared up by consensual, new agreement on international law; yet, as of now, states' positions on this question tend to be determined by subjectively perceived national interests; weightings are assigned to such differing considerations as fishing rights, exploitation of seabed resources, and naval strategic requirements.[7]

The *configuration* of influences and forces in the state's international environment comprises its set of policy problems and opportunities. In the worldwide Depression of the 1930s, when states resorted to autarkic, protective national economic policies, the sudden distortions of the world economy created unique national difficulties and unique national reactions. Japan was an island economy heavily dependent upon overseas markets and natural resources. The world depression became the occasion for national expansion to conquer the industrial resources it could not afford to purchase. The United States, relatively self-sufficient, instead undertook domestic measures in the New Deal to correct its troubles. This Japan could not do.

It is the natural need, yet not always the disposition, of policy makers to assess the international environment of their nation in a time frame

---

[7] The classic United States affirmation of the 3-mile limit, although detrimental to American coastal fishing interests, is of benefit as a general principle to United States fishing interests elsewhere and also to strategic naval interests. Yet even American policy now bends in the direction of the 12-mile limit.

that is essentially future oriented. The future, by definition, is uncertain and indeterminate—so much more pronounced, then, the craving to speculate about its potentialities and likelihoods. Is a relationship with an important ally likely to alter for reasons outside of one's control? Is a given configuration of power and influence likely to change in this or that direction? There is a natural bureaucratic impulse, common to most governments, to seek regularity and predictability in relations with other states, to reduce the hazards of chance. The greater part of international diplomacy and negotiations is designed to repair, renew, and innovate established, habitual relationships. In this fashion, changes of relations among states tend to move incrementally, often with a slowness that prompts much of it to be ignored in the press and other mass media, which, since the yellow journalism of the nineteenth century, have featured sensational, critical, immediate events rather than dwelling on deeper currents of continuity and change.[8]

Even in the best of times, however, it is a function of statecraft to anticipate, to deter, and to prevent unwanted futures; and it lies in the nature of such undramatic diplomacy that its successes in doing so are often publicly ignored, while failures, as they occur, are dramatized. It may be taken as a boon to mankind that every passing day in which nuclear war does not occur is a considerable success; yet the critical mind easily finds other things to carp about.

THE PRIMACY OF FOREIGN POLICY VERSUS THE PRIMACY OF DOMESTIC POLITICS

Among Western students of international affairs, two schools have dominated thinking about international affairs in modern times. One stresses the primacy of foreign policy and the other stresses domestic politics, as the essential source of and/or explanation of the reasons for state behavior in world politics.

[8] This aspect of news media in democratic societies—namely, their urge to dramatize confrontations—means that the media can caricature and often create the political reality that they then report. It is interesting, in America at least, to notice that sensationalism in television is least to be found at such times when commercial incentives are least; for example, Saturday and Sunday mornings. Conflict and sensationalism rear their ugly heads at peak viewer times. The media thrive on confrontations and, thus distorting reality, create new reality.

An instance out of current American arguments about the nature of American foreign policy serves to indicate the nature of distinctions between the two schools. Some current writers about American foreign policy see the impulses to sustain and enlarge America's defense establishment as arising out of an objective assessment of the strategic situation in which the nation "finds itself," and the priorities and imperatives of national security that the situation dictates. Others, however, would attribute these impulses to the structure of American corporate society, seeing the politics of defense as arising from the expansive impulses of corporate institutions and bureaucratic establishments. The first school would note that, in a world of adversary powers, including the Soviet Union, American security interests and those of America's allies entail the need for such power to deter aggression and to cope with it were deterrence to fail.

This is not the place to deal with these special contentions, but rather to see in them a current example of a very long controversy that has occurred in many nations and will not easily be stilled.

The school of primacy of foreign policy had as its original forceful theorists European writers such as Machiavelli, statesmen like Richelieu of France, and practitioners such as Bismarck, the first chancellor of imperial Germany. For them, necessities of foreign policy sprang in the first order from the tight configurations of European politics. The European states, packed together in close proximity, found themselves constantly affected by changes in configurations and relationships in and among the several states. The tendency of one or more of them to expand or to extend influence over others could set in motion changes involving and even endangering the interests of others. In such circumstances, rulers constantly scanned the international arena like alert game animals for signals of dangers and opportunities; because of such close proximity, the international theater with all its complexities tightly constrained the range of options and opportunities that states had at their disposal to protect or advance their interests. From this background developed the complex modern patterns of what came to be called the balance of power, wherein states jockey with each other, forming and breaking coalitions, engaging in occasional wars, and maintaining a high level of vigilance over their neighbors' intentions and capabilities. Cued by events in this international theater, statesmen could be tempted to so arrange domestic policies and priorities as to enhance their states' position within the whole system. In practice, this adjustment of domestic to international politics could signify an attempted subordination of important domestic political values to prime concerns of national security and the national interest (or, as it then was referred to in a system of dynastic states, *raison d'état*). Within such a society, the internal quality of politics could never be determined *in vacuo* "on its own merits"—the forms that politics and economic policy might take were heavily dependent upon external strategic considerations.

Even John Locke—the English theorist whose views on representative government decisively influenced American constitutional doctrine—noted the distinction between these foreign and domestic realms, as each affected the manner in which political power was constitutionally shared between executive and legislature. In his view, with respect to domestic matters, executive discretion was limited by lawful constraints of legislature and people; the executive's function was to carry out the laws that others made. This diffusion of power did not apply to the conduct of foreign affairs; for, Locke wrote, "what is to be done in reference to foreigners depending much upon their actions, and the variation of designs and interests, must be left in great part to the prudence of those who have this power committed to them, to be managed by the best of their skill for the advantage of the commonwealth."[9]

The cardinal assumptions entailed in this special view of the world may be summarized: first, the primacy of the nation's environment in the calculations of national statecraft; second, the primacy of national security and interest as touchstones of national political action; third, the primacy of calculations of power entailed in international action; and fourth, the need (again to quote John Marshall) for centralized executive "secrecy and despatch" in dealing with these external matters. A fifth can be added—for, in treating with this external world, which like the weather in the best of times still holds the prospect of great storms, a natural tendency to "be ready for the worst" introduced a necessary calculus of prudent pessimism. Former Secretary of State Dean Acheson once wrote:

---

[9] John Locke, *Of Civil Government,* J. M. Dent & Sons, Ltd., Publishers, London, 1943, pp. 191–192.

The judgment of nature upon error is death. We must make ourselves so strong that we shall not be caught defenseless or dangerously exposed in any possible eventuality. The future is unpredictable. Only one thing—the unexpected—can be reasonably anticipated. . . . The part of wisdom is to be prepared for what may happen, rather than to base our course upon faith in what should happen. . . . Here you can be wrong only once.[10]

As Gen. Maxwell Taylor remarked once, such prudential considerations brought to mind an old English saying, that "the soldier in time of peace is like a chimney in the summer."

This special circumstance of international hazard and constraint meant, for foreign-policy makers, that voluntary choice and the possibilities for unilateral action were highly constrained in the realm of politics outside the borders of the state. Attempts to "legislate" the nature of this outside environment could often be as futile as the commands of King Canute as he sat on his seaside throne, seeking to control the tides. Proclamations and resolutions in themselves could not ease the nature of events that occurred beyond the span of effective national influence. The engagement of diplomacy and force with the intentions and influence of others could be part of the shaping of international events, yet not in themselves be determinative. While a nation by exercise of will might commence war, it did not lie in the province of national discretion to so command peace either for itself or for others. For in the contests of many wills and influences, the national will was but one among many; a concerting of many wills, a need especially to affect the wills of adversaries, constituted a special task of strategists.

THE SUPREMACY OF DOMESTIC POLITICS

Set against this doctrine of *Realpolitik* (as the Germans came to call it) lies a contrary view, which we might here simply call the primacy of domestic politics. Here, the perspective is reversed; those who tend to espouse it are more to be found in the English-speaking world than on the European continent. Among its principal spokesmen have been such

[10] *Senate Foreign Relations Committee, Hearings on the Nomination of Dean Acheson . . .*, 81st Cong., 1st Sess., p. 20.

Americans as Thomas Jefferson (in his times of being a scholar-politician, rather than statesman), and Woodrow Wilson (before he became a President); English writers such as Richard Cobden, and John Bright, and English statesmen such as William Gladstone. Seen from this perspective, the proper priorities of the government lay in the encouragement, not of security, but of internal prosperity and welfare. The activities of government, and especially of the executive, were skeptically held suspect for possibilities of abuse; means were sought to constrain and hedge these about with restrictions. In this sanguine view, which stressed the harmony among men and nations, the sources of international conflict came from precisely those considerations that ranked so high in the thinking of *Realpolitik* advocates. The more stress placed, by foreign-policy makers, upon considerations of defense, upon an active foreign policy, and upon risks of international war, the greater the danger to internal free institutions. The fear was perceived, not so much in prospects of defeat or destruction in war, but in the national institutions designed to conduct it. In war, prerogatives and demands of the state invariably grew to great proportions at the expense of freedoms. The possession of means of defense, to deter threats, could be seen in another perspective, as among the principal causes of war. In the absence of constant struggle among states for power and influence, a harmony of interests among people would be revealed. Resources expended in the name of national security were taken away from purposes of a more benign nature—schools, public health, general internal prosperity. The pessimistic view, held by *Realpolitik* statesmen, of possible dangers emanating from the outside, could be viewed either as a mistaken set of prudential assumptions that could become self-fulfilling prophecies or as a mask to disguise claims and ambitions of a sordid character. (President Franklin D. Roosevelt, in 1941, was savagely attacked by isolationists, who claimed to see, in his executive measures taken to draw America into support of the European democracies, a disguised attempt to destroy American liberties and to become a tyrant.) Here, a liberal distrust of domestic power could combine, paradoxically, with a tendency to ignore, or to be tolerant of, the malign possibilities of external power; the realist feared external power and, fearing it, sought to augment internal national power, often at the expense of liberties. The domestic utopian, fearing internal power, sought to conceal from himself and others the possible effects of external power upon the province of his nation.

Assuming these things, utopians then tended to view the theater of international action as "naturally" or potentially benign. They further tended to think of national actions within that theater as being subject to fewer constraints and being more subject to choice and purpose, in which the range of a national option was considerable. Hence also, the liberal—supportive of democratic or representative institutions—tended to think of those great international events that occurred as being more the product of the actions of his national decision makers rather than simply as part of an interplay of such national policies and those of other nations. Thus in times of crisis or of national setbacks in world politics, national decision makers were normally to be blamed; and often, in the blaming, the wills and actions of others tended to be down-played or ignored. Thus soon after America's involvement in World War II, congressional isolationists launched a congressional investigation of the Pearl Harbor incident, to fix blame on those civil and military leaders who had "permitted" the disaster to occur; after World War I, numerous congressmen made careers exposing the machinations in the Wilson administration that led to United States involvement in that war; while during the Johnson and Nixon Administrations, congressmen sought to expose the machinations of administration officials that had led to the American decision to employ force in the Vietnam War. After the collapse of the Chinese Nationalist government in 1949, opportunist congressmen sought to blame the debacle on administration policy and on Communists in the State Department. In each instance, obviously, there was a "need to know" for the public and the nation's lawmakers, and an obvious need to hold responsible officials accountable to the public for their actions; yet in each instance, these concerns tended to blur, distort, or diminish the nature of the acute international circumstances that had contributed to the situation then deplored. As a wit remarked, during the congressional Pearl Harbor investigation, some congressmen wanted to prove that Eleanor Roosevelt had been copilot in the first Japanese attack force over Honolulu. It was not Roosevelt who handed over Eastern Europe to the Russians, but rather the Red Army that took it. Yet then, in the late 1940s, large numbers of Americans took it as received wisdom that the former was so—it accorded with a plausible "domestic" view of the Presidency, that it had such powers.

REVIEW QUESTIONS

1. In what ways does the conduct of foreign relations differ from the conduct of domestic politics?

2. What does the concept of sovereignty imply in world politics?

3. What is a "vital interest"?

4. Why do foreign-policy makers take such an interest in the capabilities of other states and not simply their policies?

5. What merits and what defects lie in the principle of national self-determination?

6. Contrast the doctrine of the primacy of foreign policy with the doctrine of the primacy of internal politics.

2 THE MEANING OF FOREIGN POLICY

Whatever one's estimate of its actual substance, the foreign policy of the United States at any given time is a complex set of national aims, programs, postures, relationships, and understandings that the nation's responsible leadership employs toward the outside world of states. Deferring for the moment the question of what principles and content may inform this policy, we should as a matter of analytic caution distinguish two crucial aspects of it: that which may be called "declaratory policy" and that which may be called "action policy." The two, in concrete circumstances, do not neatly correspond, and very important distinctions should be made between them. It is crucial that beginners should know the differences, since despite television, we still rely on the public words of policy makers, not on their private intentions or manifold actions, to tell us what they are doing.

The stated purposes of a nation, as these from time to time are spelled out by its leaders, form the backdrop for wide sets of national actions. Thus, in the 1970s, the so-called Nixon Doctrine indicates the general directions of American diplomacy, toward a lower posture in world politics. However, such pronouncements often do not exactly describe specific actions that accompany them. While policy makers necessarily take great care in the words that they use to convey such messages, often what is said publicly may differ from what is actually done. Declaratory policy (what is said about action, to explain and justify it) may cover action policy with great rhetoric, the purpose of which is to popularly legitimate it; sometimes, important yet mundane new actions or proposals are garbed in gaudy clothing that their actual nature hardly deserves. The stated purposes of American foreign policy also may contain ingredients of high aspiration that reasonable people know to be impossible of sure attainment: the goal of general and complete disarmament of all nations, the goal of a durable and universal peace, the rights of all peoples everywhere freely to choose their own governments, a world without hunger and want, and many others. Words also may act as deceptive surrogates for absent deeds; often, angry public rhetoric and bombast conceals or compensates for known inaction. So, in the time of John Foster Dulles, American rhetoric about "liberating captive nations" in Eastern Europe only partially obscured the fact that the United States government had no intention of establishing national liberation fronts in them or of rolling back the Iron Curtain. Theodore Roosevelt coined the expression "Speak softly, but carry a big stick." Sometimes it is politic to do the reverse, when to do more than loudly protest some perfidious act risks an unwanted conflict.

It sometimes may be risky or dangerous for statesmen publicly to avow the nature and purpose of actions, especially while negotiating delicate matters. In such circumstances, candor loses out to prudent evasion, silence, or even to deliberate misrepresentation. Much of what occurs in the normal relations among nations necessarily occurs in confidence; this may become acutely necessary in times of crisis. Certain ad hoc understandings arrived at during the so-called missile crisis between the United States and the Soviet Union never were publicly divulged by either state. In the interests of avoiding further dangers of thermonuclear war, each made important concessions to the other, an open admission of which would have provoked public outcries of capitulation and cowardice. (In return for Soviet promises not to reestablish nuclear sites in Cuba, the Kennedy administration evidently committed itself not to subvert the Fidel Castro regime by military assault or sponsored insurrection.)

While governments may so frame language for action policy as to make it palatable, language also may mask actual indecision, the absence of clear policy, or the existence of divided counsels. In all events, the distinction between declaratory and action policy is crucial. Emerson once wrote, "What you are thunders so that I cannot hear what you say to the contrary." But as often the reverse may be the case: What is being said may acutely interfere with our ability to perceive what is actually taking place; harsh words may conceal genuine gestures of conciliation; pleasantries may conceal hostile intentions.

The layman's first law of foreign-policy analysis then, is to admit the ambiguous relationship between words and deeds, especially in circumstances in which these are inextricably intertwined and in circumstances in which—as Max Lerner once wrote—ideas are weapons. Purists may establish for leaders high criteria of public candor that few could tolerate in their own private affairs. In a democratic and open society, where the right of dissent and the "right to know" are highly valued, the practice of secrecy, confidentiality, and persiflage may be widely abhorred. The Johnson administration, for example, was frequently attacked by critics for its "credibility gap"—namely, for an alleged dissonance between its stated claims in the Vietnam War and the assumed realities of the conflict. Yet the American adversary in that conflict, North Vietnam, is a tightly closed political system; it operates under no such domestic democratic demands whatsoever. Until 1969, for instance, it never admitted to the world that any of its troops were in South Vietnam. The asymmetrical relationship between open and closed political systems in both conflict and collaboration is one of the most acute difficulties that the United States faces in world politics. So is the management of relations between friendly open societies, when publicity uncovers antagonisms that governments mutually would prefer to conceal, in the hope of reconciliation and tactful adjustment.

THE NATIONAL INTEREST
AS FRAME OF REFERENCE

The touchstone of American foreign policy resembles that of most other sovereign nations. The aim of foreign policy is to protect and advance the interests, the welfare, and the secure survival of its land and people in a world of many other sovereign states. This high object is at once a unitary and a divisive political principle, for it assumes, on the one hand, a united community (the nation) and, on the other, a divided one (the world). Just as the principal object of American diplomacy cannot be the advancement of the welfare of the entire human race, so also it cannot be simply the advancement of particularistic domestic interests at the expense of the whole. At this intermediate position of politics, between universal and particular needs and interests, the conduct of foreign policy necessarily occurs. For this reason, also, particular policies can be simultaneously criticized for being too selfish and too altruistic, demanding of the nation that it be more than a loose aggregate of selfish (or even "selfless") individuals, while demanding that the nation's needs and requirements take precedence over those of other states. A basic requirement of the American government has been to maintain sufficient national power (with the consent of the governed) that it can deter or minimize threats of harm to its people, their public domain, and their own possessions, that it enhance the influence of the nation so that its culture and customs, freedoms and opportunities, can flourish.

That harm could be done to these values by careless or misguided pursuit of desirable foreign-policy ends is self-evident; yet much damage to such institutions may be done by foreign states and movements and by adverse developments in the international environment that surrounds the nation. In general, we might then say that the chief benign object of national policy in world politics "should" be a concern for the quality of the international environment within which the national common welfare could be pursued. The adjustment of American national needs and requirements to those of other states and peoples thus has given rise to the expression "enlightened self-interest"—a conception of selfish and sensitive interest responsive to real and imagined necessities of other states and peoples.

The multiplicity of actors in the international system of states within which American policy operates accounts both for the extraordinary

complexity of foreign policy and also for anguishing and risky decisions that have to be made among priorities of action and purpose. The United States can be understood to have a foreign policy; yet in practice policy addresses itself to many things: to major international issues, to congeries of nations, and to individual nation states in particular. The United States thus, for example, may have or may seek a general policy aiming at the nonproliferation of nuclear weapons. Yet it also has a policy toward Germany, one toward Japan, one toward India, one toward France; and each of these nations has sets of policies, including those that pertain to nuclear arms.

The necessity of relating such bilateral relations to other states or groups of states to general objects of American policy and to relations with other states imposes on policy makers problems of acute intellectual complexity; sometimes these are agonizing either-or choices. (So, currently, a United States *Realpolitik* rapprochement with Communist China risks serious deterioration of relations with other friendly states— India and Japan, for example—or sets in motion unwished-for policies on the part of other adversaries—the Soviet Union, for example.) Conjecturing about the likely effects of specific hypothetical policies upon other desired ends of national interest is normally the source of greatest disputations in the policy-making machinery; no choice is cost free, and so it is that quite frequently the most difficult choices must be made between or among quite meritorious ends and objects. Equally, policy makers must anticipate that side effects and by-products of national policies will necessarily accompany the attainment of some specific policy goal; often, in retrospect, unintended consequences of policy come to have greater import than the specific policy itself. The United States decision to demilitarize Japan after VJ Day, for instance, meant that thereafter Japan and Japanese security needs had to be protected by American power. This was a logical and crucial consequence of a benign policy, yet few American policy makers at the time realized it.

One illustration of this difficulty comes readily to mind in the recent admission of Communist China to the United Nations. This American object has a rationale shared by many other states: notably, to lessen tension with one of America's most militant Asian adversaries; to bring China out of its belligerent posture of isolation in hopes that its militance might be thereby diminished by its broader exposure to other states. Yet

Communist China's membership entails clear risks and prices; nothing is cost free. The prospect of the forcible incorporation of Taiwan by mainland China after its expulsion from the international community risks the loss of self-rule to millions of Taiwanese and as well their subjection to totalitarian rule. Communist China as a UN member also complicates United Nations multilateral peacekeeping work in areas such as the Middle East, where China's "allies" include militant extremist groups.

POLICY AND "NO-POLICY POLICY"

It is a characteristic of a great power, which the United States is, that its capabilities and influence are present and effective in all major questions of international politics, whether or not it wishes that this be so. This characteristic yields a paradox with respect to policy: "having no policy" with regard to a major international issue itself constitutes a policy. The consequences of American action or inaction today are seen by many to greatly affect the real or imagined outcome of all external issues. In the late 1940s, for example, it seemed extremely likely that Mao Tse-tung's Communist-led insurgency in China would establish effective control of both the Chinese mainland and Formosa; it became therefore the announced policy of the Truman administration, with respect to this possibility, to "let the dust settle" before determining its relationship to this new fact of life. Such a posture of "wait and see" entailed a willful suspension of American influence over events in circumstances in which it had previously been very considerable. This new posture, to be sure, was quickly ended by an unprovoked Communist attack upon the Republic of Korea in 1950. Yet before then, of course, this Acheson-Truman formula, widely attacked by domestic critics as willful abandonment of the Chiang Kai-shek Nationalist government, entered into Asian equations of force and influence.

Strong domestic pressures repeatedly are brought upon the American government to intervene in circumstances of international conflict, often without avail. But when American influence is then withheld, the United States has rarely been spared the paradoxical accusation that its neutrality (or passivity) itself constitutes "intervention" and action. A cautious withholding of American aid to the Nigerian government and insurrectionists alike, in the recent Biafran war, was widely interpreted as evidence of America's tacit support of the stronger side, namely, the Nigerian federal government. So, too, American refusal to aid African

movements and states to punish South Africa for its ruthless *apartheid* practices has been taken by some as evidence of "racist" partisanship.

At a much earlier stage in American history, in its formative years, this problem arose most acutely during the French Revolution, in early stages of conflict between revolutionary France and Britain. Domestic opponents of President George Washington's policy of neutrality accused the Federalist administration of partiality to Britain and of opposition to a cause that many idealists—Jefferson included—saw as advancing the welfare of humanity in general. A policy of neutrality thus was condemned as one of partisanship.

American history is strewn with such instances, and the problem has not disappeared nor has it been intellectually resolved. In Latin America, where the question of United States intervention has long been passionately disputed, it well may be argued, on the basis of innumerable case histories of Latin turmoil, that *anything* done, or not done, by the United States with respect to Latin America constitutes intervention—the withholding of aid to dissident groups of rebels, the withdrawal of aid to an established government (the Batista regime in Cuba, for instance), the proffering of aid to an incumbent regime (Betancourt's government in Venezuela, for instance), the withdrawal of economic investments or the introduction of them, the giving or withholding of military assistance to one or another state. One feature of Franklin D. Roosevelt's Good Neighbor Policy in Latin America, namely, its fairly consistent refusal to directly intervene in the internal affairs of *any* Latin-American state, resulted in a consequent unusual stability of most Latin-American regimes, chiefly authoritarian ones, during most of the 1930s and through World War II. Such are the paradoxical dilemmas of great powers: their potential influence, applied or withheld, nevertheless in all circumstances is reputed to bear upon all situations within its possible reach, and thus the "isolation" or the authentic neutrality of a great power is an impossibility.

INCREMENTAL VERSUS
SHOCK DIPLOMACY

It is a current characteristic of American foreign policy that most of the time its central strategic components and its tactical activities develop incrementally; most actions are routine, predictable, and lacking in surprise. Change, as it occurs, does so in acts of renewing, repairing, or improving existing relationships or commencing new ones that correspond to familiar patterns. Diplomacy, as someone has suggested, thus normally resembles more the art of gardening than of bulldozing. It entails nurturing, sustaining, and repairing of old friendships and the cultivation of new ones; the careful management of old and familiar situations of adversary relationships.

In part this is so because of a natural human quest for reasonable predictability in arenas within which men can then with some certitude plan their affairs. Otherwise, when the general political universe is very uncertain, provisional, and shadowed with portents of total alteration, psychological insecurity mounts to fear. A central defect of the foreign-policy postures of post-Bismarckian imperial Germany (once the old bugbear of European politics) is said to have been its mercurial character—shifting unpredictably in moods, affections, friendships, and animosities—so that few saw it as a dependable element in the stability of a European order. Arrogance and chauvinism were involved in this diplomatic defect; but, basically, its unstable fickleness constituted the difficulty. By way of contrast, the elephantine predictability of British foreign policy at the same time (England then, a British statesman once said, had no friends but only interests) was a stabilizing and unthreatening element in European affairs.

The quest for predictability alone does not explain this cautious preference for incremental rather than radical changes. In addition, the style of sudden diplomacy and swift alteration of objectives, even when necessity seems to require it, entails very great dangers, including those of unwanted scenarios leading to thermonuclear abysses, to loss of crucial confidence among allies, and to confusion of both friends and adversaries concerning American intentions. Great cleavages may develop within public opinion, which when startled by new events becomes excitable.

DOCTRINES OF AMERICAN DIPLOMACY

American statecraft periodically fashions strategic doctrines and principles representing current goals of American policies. Some exhort, some warn, some catalog specific items of immediate national concern. Since the early nineteenth century, American usage has favored issuance of such doctrines, since Monroe first fashioned his great warning to the European powers in 1823. In recent times, the Truman Doctrine and the Eisenhower Doctrine flashed to others American signals of concern about major international problems. In World War I, Woodrow Wilson's famous Fourteen Points served the same purpose as did Roosevelt's (and Churchill's) Atlantic Charter in 1941. The Nixon Doctrine now dominates the scene.

Such pronouncements serve as indicators of current moods, aspirations, and policies. Some, like the Monroe Doctrine of 1823, have had surprising longevity as vital statements of concern and purpose. Others, like the Truman Doctrine, although designed to cope with a geographically finite problem (namely, the power balance in the Eastern Mediterranean), by their universal language came to command great significance as rationale for broader American purposes.

Such doctrines in themselves are of limited utility, however, in revealing underlying bases of the nation's foreign policies or the kinds of attitudes that predispose Americans to act as they do. They do not in themselves suggest the mainsprings or motives of American behavior.

THE DUALITY OF AMERICAN PERCEPTIONS OF WORLD POLITICS

Through time, and since the beginning of the American nation, many Americans have shared a paradoxical duality about the external environment surrounding their country. This duality has not diminished as American power and influence have surged to the fore in world politics.

On the one hand, there has been a consistent and ebullient outward thrust of American interests in the external world, which in the nineteenth century manifested itself in actual territorial expansion of the American nation itself. In the twentieth century, the thrust assumed different forms than mere expansion of the American state itself: a restless mobility in a shrinking world, in which old frontiers had closed and new frontiers assumed quite different guises. This expansionist spirit could be seen, not merely in the specific realm of politics, but also in business affairs (the corporate life) of the nation and in the aspirations of private American citizens. In a simple psychological sense, one might describe this American spirit as a concern for a "world of wide horizons." Whether the aspiration referred to economics (the idea of the "open door"), to politics (a world of "free societies"), or simply to the rights of individual Americans ("freedom to travel"), it has been perhaps more aspirational than factual; for now, as earlier, the number of people lucky to live in open societies in the world comprise a minority of the human race; the right to travel (regarded by most Americans as absolute) is absolutely denied by certain other governments—Communist regimes especially— to populations comprising the vast majority of the people of the world. As an economic reality, an open door to investment and trade likewise is limited both by practices of the great state-trading nations of the Communist world and by pragmatic policies of many other nations.

In this sense, there has been a restless American concern with the constraints of this external world on their movement and their rights as citizens. This concern may simply be explained as a carryover of their democratic rights at home. A restless dissatisfaction with constraints is today a monopoly of no class or race in America, although the restlessness turns momentarily inward upon the character of American domestic institutions. It is not surprising that a democratic people should then wish to enjoy a world environment congenial to such freedoms; in World War II, when America was faced with prospects that Asia and Europe might both be dominated by contrary principles of restraint and compression, President Roosevelt formulated his version of American goals in that war as the Four Freedoms—Freedom of Speech, Freedom of Religion, Freedom from Want, and Freedom from Fear.

Accompanying this ebullience about the nature of the external world, however, there has long been a persistent psychological sensitivity to certain kinds of political changes in the external environment that are deemed adverse to American safety. While we might attribute the origins of such sensitivity to psychological factors, yet so to characterize it is not to diminish its importance. Thus we have a strange duality, compounded of optimistic aspirations and anxieties.

We should observe this sensitivity in the course of American history, a continuity of latent attitude *even during times when it is not at the forefront of public attention.* It accounts, especially in times of great international crisis, for the supposed "instability of American moods" about their foreign affairs. The latency of this popular mood must be noted even in times of calm. An example may suffice.

In the late spring of 1940, after the German victory over France in Europe, the panic that spread through America was far more profound than a sympathetic reaction to the brutal subjection of a friendly democratic nation. It reflected a sudden fear (after two decades of American isolation and slackened concern with national defense) that America was defenseless and that it was the next likely target of Nazi aggression. A Gallup Poll taken at the time indicated that nearly two-thirds of the American public was convinced that Hitler intended to seize territory on this side of the Atlantic. As one writer pointed out at the time: "There has suddenly flared up a panic about our defenseless state—as if somebody was on the point of invading us or attacking this continent." [1] In calm hindsight, how exaggerated such fears were! In point of fact, in 1940, Hitler had hardly enough resources to consider an invasion of the British Isles, much less a trans-Atlantic invasion of North America; to him, quite rightly, such American fears were absurd. Much as he held American democracy in contempt, Hitler at that time had neither the capabilities, nor the wish, to conquer America. His objectives, established in *Mein Kampf* and in subsequent action consistent with the book, were exclusively "Continental."

This instance of intense yet unwarranted anxiety (and there are many others like it) should not cause us to dismiss them as mere "states of mind." American demagogues and political hypochondriacs often roast real marshmallows over imaginary fires. (Never were words of a poet so politically abused, as were those of John Donne in the typewriters of foreign-policy pundits in the 1940s and 1950s. Ernest Hemingway's novel *For Whom the Bell Tolls* touched this off: the message being that a threat to any nation anywhere from anyone is a threat to all nations: the bell "tolls for thee.") But the fires we speak of here have been real ones; and the object of reasoned national intelligence is to take measure of their potentialities rather than to dispute their existence. So also, it is essential in foreign-policy matters never to ignore the existence of such traits and moods in others, notably in America's adversaries. It should not be a principal object of American foreign policy therapeutically to alleviate anxieties of adversaries, while leaving one's own real interests unattended. But several vast miscalculations in the recent past have

---

[1] John T. Flynn, quoted in William Langer and S. Everett Gleason, *The Challenge to Isolation,* Harper & Row, Publishers, New York, 1952, p. 479. At that time, only 30 percent of the public, according to the polls, retained "belief" in an Allied victory.

been made by policy makers precisely because of an underestimation of this factor. It was not a purpose of Gen. Douglas MacArthur's UN forces in North Korea in 1950 to sweep on into Manchuria when they suddenly ranged victoriously near the Chinese border. But evidently Chinese Communist leaders saw the matter differently and very anxiously; observing the proximity of American capabilities, rather than heeding American intentions, they chose to intervene in the war, thus confounding MacArthur's strategic assumptions. So also, Khrushchev's Cuban missile folly in 1962 (which later caused his successors to brand him as an "adventurer") wholly miscalculated the intensity of the American response.

Some today deplore strong anxiety expressed about the hypothetical spread of Castro's communism in the traditional area of American acute sensitivity, the Caribbean. The argument here often is that such anxiety represents a kind of unwarranted and undifferentiated anticommunism. But the anxiety in fact belongs to a more comprehensive category of concern about American security. From such a perspective, however rational it may be, Latin-American communism, linked to interests of a great non-Hemispheric adversary power, readily fits into a traditional Monroe Doctrine frame of reference. It belongs in a long chain of prospective perceived threats in that area from innumerable non-American sources: Great Britain, Spain, Napoleonic France, the Holy Alliance, Maximilian and Napoleon III, imperial Germany (recall the famous Zimmerman note of 1917), Japan, and Nazi Germany. None of these were Communist threats; each of them in greater or lesser degree was perceived by policy makers as posing threats to American security. It may not have been an object of French foreign policy during the American Civil War to establish in Maximilian's Mexican regime a beachhead from which to invade the United States; but prudent American statesmen in Lincoln's time, even when keenly aware of terrible costs of the Civil War, still were moved to bang out tunes on the old calliope of the Monroe Doctrine; and the French government quickly heeded their warnings. Axiomatic behavior—the known kinds of responses that states habitually make to familiar challenges—is one branch of foreign-policy knowledge that needs best to be learned.

It may then be seen as a function of foreign policy, not to succumb to such anxieties but to seek to deflect them by means that diminish or preclude the possibilities both of real danger of thermonuclear war and of poorly controllable public passion.

REVIEW QUESTIONS

1. What is the relationship between declaratory policy and action policy?

2. What is the meaning of the "national interest"? As a test of policy, can it ever be used to decide what ought to be done in concrete cases or is it simply a judgmental frame of reference?

3. In foreign-policy making, what considerations ought to come into play to determine the degree of candor and openness versus the degree of secrecy and confidentiality?

4. If both action and inaction of the United States in world politics affect outcomes of international conflicts, is the idea of intervention and interventionism therefore meaningless?

3 THE CONSTITUTION AND FOREIGN AFFAIRS

The experience of the Vietnam War was largely responsible for long-drawn-out debate in the United States—a debate that has strong constitutional undertones; the principal questions entailed in it concern the location of authority to determine the broad outlines of American foreign policy. Two chief questions posed are: (1) Is the power of the American President over questions of war and peace excessive? (2) Should and can Presidential control over the use and deployment of the armed forces be curtailed? Yet there are many other related questions; some of these pertain to the general question: How should foreign policy *be* made? Who should participate? What should be the criteria by which participation should be determined? Are democratic institutions threatened by strong executive powers in foreign relations? Are democratic states able to act in world politics as purposefully as states organized along more authoritarian lines? What is more important to the welfare of the nation: the ability to swiftly and certainly respond to external challenges or the need to ground national actions in world politics upon broad "consent of the governed"?

THE AUTHORITY TO ACT

Among the constitutional issues perennially facing the American nation since 1789, the nature of authority to conduct foreign policy has been a hardy perennial. The fundamental questions it entails today closely resemble those that concerned the founding fathers. In nearly two centuries, major changes in the character of the United States Constitution have occurred in consequence of judicial interpretation; yet there is recurring revival of the questions related to how the powers over foreign relations are to be focused, diffused, checked, or made plenary. The occasions of their salience are in times when major changes in the direction of foreign policy occur, especially in times of crisis, when the nation faces either the prospect of war or war itself and when the public is deeply divided about "what to do," in swiftly changing international circumstances.

The constitutional question is indifferent to the specific nature of the decisions themselves. But the central concerns usually pertain to concrete matters of war and peace, the security of the nation, and to ways in which national actions taken in the international arena in response to crises, in turn may feed back and affect the distribution of powers and authority in domestic life and impose costs upon the nation. There are few other nations in the world in which such political questions of choice, arising in concrete circumstances, become translated into constitutional ones; there also is no indication that this constitutional issue, perennially raised, can ever be subject to definitive solution.

A constitutional lawyer, E. S. Corwin, once remarked that the Constitution from the beginning has been an "invitation to struggle for the privilege of conducting foreign policy." This is so since, while the basic law of the nation is set clearly upon principles of the separation and distribution of powers and of limitations upon power, the effective carrying out of basic lines of foreign policy requires unified control and guidance.

THE SEPARATION OF POWERS

The idea of the separation of powers—legislative, executive, and judicial—was a common constitutional principle acknowledged by the makers of the Constitution and one that John Locke, the English liberal political theorist, forcefully had propounded. The principle was based upon a conception of representative government, in which lawmakers, elected by and accountable to their electors, would establish laws which then an executive would faithfully carry out. In this manner, popular control, by way of representatives, would justify popular obligation to obey the law, and government would thus be based upon the consent of the governed, to whom their elected representatives were accountable. This theory was based upon Locke's view of government as a limited, convenient, and reasonable contrivance made by men in contract to each other. The executive was therefore accountable to those whose elected servant he was.

Locke saw, however, in foreign affairs, a political condition that differed greatly from that *within* his commonwealth—one that required in the external realm a fusion and centralization of govermental powers, rather than their limitation and separation:

> For though in a commonwealth the members of it are distinct persons . . . in reference to one another, and, as such, are governed by the laws of the society, yet, in reference to the rest of mankind, they make one body, which is, as every member of it before was, still in the state of Nature with the rest of mankind, so that the controversies that happen between any man of the society with those that are out of it are managed by the public, and an injury done to a member of their body engages the whole in the reparation of it. So that under this consideration the whole community is one body in the state of Nature in respect of all other states. . . .

> This, therefore, contains the power of war and peace, leagues and alliances, and all the transactions with all persons and communities without the commonwealth, and may be called federative if any one pleases. . . .

> Though this federative power in the well or ill management of it be of great moment to the commonwealth, yet it is as much less capable to be directed

by antecedent, standing, positive laws than the executive, and so must necessarily be left to the prudence and wisdom of those whose hands it is in, to be managed for the public good. . . . [For] what is to be done in reference to foreigners depending much upon their actions, and the variation of designs and interests, must be left in great part to the prudence of those who have this power committed to them, to be managed by the best of their skill for the advantage of the commonwealth.[1]

While Locke's thought generally is regarded as having been of decisive influence upon the American Constitution, nevertheless this aspect of it, on the concentration of political power, was significantly blurred by the drafters of the Constitution. The resulting constitutional ambiguities have remained ever since. In the American Constitution, the power to declare war is vested in Congress; the power to make treaties (including treaties of peace) is shared by the President with the Senate; the power to act as commander in chief of the armed forces is given to the President, while the funding of the defense and foreign-policy establishments is in the hands of Congress. The power of Congress to levy customs on imported goods and to legislate on matters of immigration and naturalization is its own, even though it thereby establishes the nation's commercial and cultural policies with respect to the outside world. (The President's own authority to act as the chief diplomatic agent in the nation's dealings with others was established not by the Constitution but by subsequent practice and judicial interpretation.)

The principal reason for this blurring of Locke's view of the executive is to be seen in the fact that most of the Constitution drafters, themselves poachers incompletely converted into gamekeepers, had been leaders of the American rebellion against Crown authority. The notion of a strong executive symbolized the very authority they had successfully rebelled against. In foreign affairs, the Crown (royal authority) had involved the Colonies in European and in global wars, for purposes often obscurely relatable to the immediate interests of the colonists. The postindependence leadership thus installed a suspicion of British alliance politics and of royal prerogatives in the very executive institutions they devised for themselves. Memories of ceaseless struggles in colonial governments between popularly chosen legislatures and royally appointed governors

---

[1] John Locke, *Of Civil Government*, J. M. Dent & Sons, Ltd., Publishers, London, 1943, chap. XII, pp. 191–192.

had so intensified this prejudice against executive authority that around it they hedged many constraints. This American executive was to be elected, not hereditary; native, not foreign; and of limited, not indefinite term. Yet such mechanical constraints hardly affected this disposition further to check its adult prerogatives even before it was born. In consequence, ever since, institutional jealousies and fears of encroachments of powers have attended nearly every major reshifting of American foreign policy, especially when strong executive leadership has come into play; and on frequent occasions the American reputation as a credible actor in international affairs has thereby been severely questioned.

It is one thing to understand the historical origins of a constitutional "understanding," arrangement, or impasse; it is another to inquire into the considerations that lie at the heart of the matter and that are enduring dilemmas of American politics.

Let us first look into the argument, advanced then and now, for checking presidential authority in the field of foreign affairs, hedging it about with constraints; for it is a powerful one.

LEASHING THE PRESIDENT

In a most general sense, two aspects of democratic politics always exist together, yet must be known as quite distinct. One is the aspect of *governing,* which is the art of making authoritative decisions and of choosing among alternatives in such a way as to make choice effective and enduring. The other aspect is that of *representing* those who will have to live with such choices and who most likely will have to pay, sometimes even with their lives, for decision(s) made.

In democratic theory, neither of these two can be sacrificed to the other. Yet of these twin features, the latter strongly appeals to our democratic instincts. The ordinary man, after all, is the one in whose interests public affairs are conducted; for him to consent to actions proposed or taken would seem self-evident and would also require, even if indirectly, his participation in the choice—the more so, since his involvement in the consequences of action taken is likely to be very considerable. Also, to have any significance, rational public deliberation must take place under conditions in which the general range of choices are revealed and clear and in which logically also the backdrop of conditions giving rise to the need for choices is known. *Consent* therefore needs a degree of openness of knowledge of what was actually occurring, of what options were being actually considered, and of what in fact is being decided. Were a gulf to develop between an autonomous, authoritarian executive (together with its bureaucracy) and the public and its legislators, so that actions taken by the former were shrouded in secrecy or misrepresented, there would develop not only a "credibility gap," endangering constitutional understandings, but even a constitutional crisis entailing a breach of faith, a disruption of a delicate and crucial understanding. Furthermore, so this argument would go, an executive grown accustomed to great latitudes of discretionary power might well risk engagement in adventures possibly alien to the actual needs and interests of the nation—in extreme instances even harnessing the nation to fantasies of the executive imagining (a likelihood not infrequently to be seen in historical circumstances, including rather recent ones). Thus we have the civics-book picture of citizenry, alert to affairs, eager to check excesses, and needful to be consulted and accurately informed. Needless to say, these civics-book qualities of the public applied even more cogently to its elected legislators, who were even more needful of continuing rapport with the executive.

In the twentieth century, this argument seemingly gained in cogency and urgency, as the powers of government generally gained a reach and a strength they never before had enjoyed and as the resources at the disposal of the government grew as each new task was placed upon it, in each phase of international crisis the nation encountered. The complexity of the executive institutions devised to deal with the nation's security problems became as ponderous as the complexity of the issues with which they dealt. The agencies stretched over into the private institutions of the nation's life—into its corporate business firms, its universities, and its political system. The American employees in, for example, either the United States embassy in Stockholm or the one in New Delhi by 1970 numbered as many as the personnel of the American Department of State in 1900. The Central Intelligence Agency (CIA), with as many as 28,000 operatives, itself exceeded in numbers, if not intelligence, the total student population of many a major American university. It was also a characteristic of the executive branch, in cold-war crisis diplomacy, to engage in actions that by their very nature were shrouded in secrecy, yet bore directly upon potentialities of war and peace. These—in the conventional wisdom of Locke and Jefferson—were matters to be controlled by legislators elected by the people and accountable to them. Thus covert actions, taken in swiftness or calculated deliberation, in the name of American foreign policy and American national interests, could and did entail the use of force against or within other nations, the subvention or subversion of insurgencies against foreign governments, the condoning or resistance to coups d'état in far-off places. These developments sometimes transpired with little or no consultation afforded even the committees of Congress charged with oversight of executive branch actions. A sequence of such actions could shape and determine the general course of the nation's movement in international affairs; in moments of crisis, it could commit the nation to a situation of conflict with no particular prior consultation with Congress. (So it was, for example, that President Harry S. Truman in 1950 committed United States ground troops to combat in Korea without even prior consultation with congressional *leaders* and without asking Congress for a declaration of war, as the Constitution apparently requires.) In this fashion, while amenities of congressional budgetary authorizations might be observed to pay for executive "adventures," the initiative and thrust of action, however justified, would lie in the executive branch and not in the Congress—much less in the public.

Other compelling considerations were set against these democratic requirements of openness, public deliberation, and legislative consent; and often those Americans who criticized the executive for constitutional abuses did so with reference to constitutional norms that did not similarly constrain other nations in the conduct of their foreign relations. The norms of state behavior in world politics were not those that American constitutional principles alone could dictate.

We might summarize these compelling considerations under two criteria, which Chief Justice John Marshall, the greatest American jurist of the nineteenth century, called the criteria of "secrecy and despatch" and a further criterion, that of consistency of purpose and design.

OPEN AND CLOSED DIPLOMACY

Just as openness is a procedural virtue of democracies, secrecy (and confidentiality, its euphemistic twin) is the norm of state relations. In the best of normal times, transactions between friendly governments are reciprocally confidential, except when otherwise mutually agreed. American diplomacy in such dealings would become impossible under unilaterally imposed requirements of publicity and openness. In bargaining between states, a constitutional principle of openness forced upon one, but not on the other, with respect to its behavior and strategies, would come to resemble an asymmetrical poker game in which the hand of one was concealed and that of the other open. For what is divulged to one's democratic public is universally knowable, while what is concealed from a domestic public is also concealable from the rest of the world.

Nor is this simply a matter affecting merely the self-interests of the American democracy in bargaining and diplomacy. Full publicity given to transactions with other states also could inhibit the bargaining flexibility and candor of other states—partners and adversaries alike—which themselves have domestic considerations to bear in mind and other constituencies to consider. At the Paris peace conference in 1919, President Woodrow Wilson—an advocate of "open covenants, openly arrived at" as a basic principle of relations among nations—quickly discovered that in practice the principle was foolish; a few days after his arrival in Paris as America's chief negotiator, he surrounded the American embassy with marines and clamped down tight secrecy on his dealings with the British, French, and others.

Such considerations bear on the normal and peaceable transactions among states; yet they bear more crucially upon adversary relations and especially on relations with closed societies that do not follow the democratic rules of the game.

In the twentieth century, especially after the totalitarian revolutions of fascism and communism, entirely new challenges were posed to democratic and even authoritarian traditionalist states, with respect to matters of foreign affairs. The novel techniques of totalitarian dictatorships posed these challenges. In dealings with other nations, totalitarian states operated essentially on two levels: that of formal relations with other governments and that of "people-to-people diplomacy," in which by techniques of subversion, infiltration, and internal warfare, their own interests could be advanced, governments overthrown, and whole societies disrupted or otherwise transformed. On this latter level, the clandestine character of activity was especially notable; it transcended simple espionage, and it rarely could be countered by simple, conventional diplomatic means. Even in times of nominal peace, such techniques were practiced. In combination with other devices—of terror, "normal" diplomacy, and military force—these operational weapons became normal auxiliaries of foreign policy. It also was the nature of the new managed societies that the totalitarians confronted "open" democratic or quasi-democratic societies with "closed" ones, in varying degrees hermetically sealed off from significant contacts with the outside world. Opposition groups within them were eliminated or repressed. Information was managed; opinion was centrally manipulated. In dealings with such closed societies, American foreign policy was faced with acute dilemmas. Traditionally abhorring clandestine methods of politics, of information gathering, and of intelligence, the American political system during and after World War II commenced itself to adopt such techniques for its own purposes. After the war, the improvised wartime Office of Strategic Services, under Gen. William Donovan, became permanently established in the Central Intelligence Agency (CIA), having as its dual purpose the clandestine conduct of political operations and clandestine intelligence gathering and evaluation. Such activities, shielded necessarily and logically both from the American public and from adversaries and friends alike, posed novel forms of political problems for a democracy. An entire range of governmental activity became shielded from public scrutiny.

In the cold war, such novel American activities included the covert intervention in internal affairs of other countries, even on occasion the overthrow of regimes; the arming of defensive paramilitary organizations; internal propaganda; and even violent attacks upon individuals. New Left critics in the 1960s made the CIA one of its prime "establishment" targets, alleging it to be a device for maintaining "reactionary" regimes or overthrowing "progressive" ones. Yet countless CIA-sponsored activities in foreign affairs entailed the support of revolutionary movements and leftist causes, which a relatively conservative American Congress never would have condoned had such support been public knowledge. It was conservatives like Sen. Barry Goldwater who complained of this, before the New Left did. One major revolutionary figure and "theorist," Franz Fanon, befriended by the CIA during the Algerian

War, was brought by the agency back to Washington, where he died of cancer in an army hospital. The very nature of clandestine activity obscured it from public scrutiny, and there was always the danger that these enterprises might even escape from Presidential control and surveillance. Here, a major problem arose for American democracy; namely, the accountability of a political arm of the American government exempt from normal scrutiny of congressional committees.

By a process of "unilateral disarmament," the United States might have foresworn such techniques, which by now were common property of nearly all major nations and which were powerful devices of powerful adversaries. Yet in so doing, it would have risked depriving itself of means by which it could know of and often accurately assess important developments in those nations that drastically curtailed information about their nature, capabilities, and intentions. Ironically, the relatively open nature of the American political system made it relatively easy for totalitarian states to reply upon overt, rather than clandestine, intelligence in their assessment of American capabilities and intentions—far easier than for open societies to learn by any means about them. Such a self-denial on the American part, by unilaterally depriving its statesmen of basic knowledge on which to act rationally, might have contributed to irrationally designed and dangerous responses to international crises.

An illustration of this was to be seen at the time of the famous U-2 incident in 1960—when the Soviet Union revealed that an American intelligence surveillance plane had been shot down while covertly patrolling Russian skies for photographic information about Russian strategic installations. Then, as now, it was far easier for Soviet intelligence to find out what was going on in the United States' strategic force development than vice versa, if only by reading unclassified governmental reports, congressional debates and hearings, and strategic literature. Such normal access to information available to anyone never could have been grounds for American outrage at Russian surveillance; yet the American violation of Soviet airspace—a compensatory intelligence crutch—had drastic political repercussions. A gentlemanly restraint in such covert intelligence operations on the American part might have avoided such risks, only to endure others—for instance, that of being in the dark with respect to Soviet capabilities and framing defense policy simply on hunches and guesses. Such blindness could lead to exaggerated fears, more likely than to complacent confidence. To meet an unknown threat, any amount of defense is warranted.

Thus it was that secrecy became institutionalized in the American political system.

A DERANGEMENT OF CONSTITUTIONAL POWERS?

In general terms, we may speak of two distinct types of constitutional impasses, both of which might set President and Congress, President and Senate, at loggerheads with each other. As can be seen readily, both often arise with respect to the same kinds of political questions. The first entails the paralysis of national action in consequence of legislative negation of executive actions or legislative constraints on executive options and discretion in dealing with foreign states. The second pertains to executive determinations and decisions taken in defiance of strong legislative or public opposition or executive action covertly negating strong public or congressional opinion. In both kinds of instances, a breach of trust can generate many side effects in the political system.

A derangement of powers in democracies can be seen in those situations in which public and legislative opinions become so sharply hostile as to imperil executive functions. Walter Lippmann, in his *Public Philosophy,* once called this the "malady of democratic states," a functional derangement of power in which the legislature, itself incompetent to exercise the art of governing, either preempts executive power or systematically shackles or nullifies it. Public opinion at its worst could become a "massive negative imposed at critical junctures when a new course of policy needed to be set." When foreign affairs become alien, everything connected with it is usually "dangerous, painful, disagreeable, and exhausting." In Lippmann's words:

> At critical junctures, when the stakes are high, the prevailing mass opinion will impose what amounts to a veto upon changing the course on which the government at the time is proceeding. Prepare for war in times of peace? No. It is bad to raise taxes, to unbalance the budget, to take men away from their schools or their jobs, to provoke the enemy. Intervene in a developing conflict? No. Avoid the risk of war. Withdraw from the area of conflict? No. The adversary must not be appeased. Reduce your claims on the area? No.

Righteousness cannot be compromised. Negotiate a compromise peace as soon as the opportunity presents itself? No. The aggressor must be punished. Remain armed to enforce the dictated settlement? No. The war is over.[2]

The famous French observer of American affairs, Alexis de Tocqueville, was equally critical of American democracy in this respect:

It is most especially in the conduct of foreign relations that democratic governments appear to me to be decidedly inferior to governments carried on upon different conditions. . . . Good sense may suffice to direct the ordinary course of society; and among people whose education has been provided for, the advantages of democratic liberty in the internal affairs of the country may more than compensate for the evils inherent in a democratic government. But such is not always the case in the mutual relations of foreign nations.

Foreign policy politics demand scarcely any of those qualities which a democracy possesses; and they require, on the contrary, the perfect use of almost all those faculties in which it is deficient. Democracy is favourable to the increase of the internal resources of the State; it tends to diffuse a moderate independence; it promotes the growth of public spirit. . . . But a democracy is unable to regulate the details of an important undertaking, to persevere in a design, and to work out its execution in the presence of serious obstacles. It cannot combine its measures with secrecy, and it will not await their consequences with patience. . . . The propensity [of] democracies . . . [is] to obey the impulse of passion rather than the suggestions of prudence, and to abandon a mature design for the gratification of a momentary caprice.[3]

These comments, which now seem pertinent to contemporary American problems, were on de Tocqueville's part quite conjectural; for the time he wrote them was one of very little American activity in international politics. As he wrote, "The foreign policy of the United States is reduced by its very nature to await the chances of the future history of

[2]Walter Lippmann, *The Public Philosophy,* Mentor Books, New York, 1955, pp. 22–23.
[3]Alexis de Tocqueville, *Democracy in America,* Oxford University Press, New York, 1955, pp. 160–161.

the nation, and for the present it consists more in abstaining from interference than in exerting its activity."

The pathological possibilities in this constitutional relationship since de Tocqueville wrote of them are many—some are unavoidable. A cautious President, fearing lest he lose congressional or public support, yet aware of harsh necessities in an emerging situation, might proceed too slowly in response to crisis, substituting improvisation for strategy, seeking to avoid circumstances in which his plans collided with conventional public wisdom. As for Franklin D. Roosevelt in the 1930s, the temptation to resort to deception, acting in one way while talking in another, would be great. A President, convinced of the need for unpopular strategic action yet fearful of congressional opposition, might by demagoguery exaggerate purposes and excite opinion beyond the actual needs of circumstances, simply to overcome congressional inertia. Compromising between foreign necessities and contrary domestic opinion, a President might chart a course "half-way between," risking in consequence an expediential mix of policy inadequate to external challenge yet nevertheless anathema to important parts of the public either for its supposed insufficiency or for its supposed excessiveness. A President aware of congressional or public pitfalls and delays were he to risk seeking congressional sanction for his measures, might "act now, consult later," presenting the legislature with *faits accomplis,* which it could reject only at risk of imperiling the nation's international reputation.

Rapid changes in the international scene could enormously foreshorten the time span in which decisions had to be made. (An American Congress during the Napoleonic Wars deliberated eight years over questions of war and peace, before the War of 1812; yet, for example, President Truman, faced with swift Communist aggression in Korea in 1950, virtually overnight committed American troops to combat with absolutely no prior consultation with Congress.) In even more significant hypothetical circumstances, as in the case of possible nuclear attack, Presidential decisions risking millions of American lives might have to be made on a moment's notice.

CONGRESSIONAL AUTHORITY

The pathology could also exist in Congress. "Have a cat," Mark Twain once wrote, "sit on a hot stove, and it will be absolutely certain it will not sit on one again; but then, it will not sit on a cold one either." A legislature, remembering real or fancied Presidential excesses, could so chain and constrain the executive in its discretionary powers, as to tether it to rigid responses to external situations, demanding inflexible responses to circumstances where flexibility was required. In some instances, it could (as did the American Senate in 1919) explicitly repudiate Presidential treaty commitments to other states and thus present to the world the picture of a nation not to be trusted in its international dealings. In other instances, for ideological or other reasons, it could press upon the executive branch demands for foreign-policy actions that might endanger relations with other states and even lead to war. In the 1950s belated congressional reaction to Roosevelt's secret wartime agreements with the Soviet Union led to the proposed but defeated Bricker amendment to the Constitution, severely inhibiting the President's authority to make executive agreements with other states.

One lesson learned too well, others could be forgotten. The Constitution was a blunt weapon, even a boomerang, when employed in specific contentions over public policy. Whose ox was to be gored? In point of fact, since the Constitution concerned itself with the *distribution* of powers, rather than with their exercise in particular circumstances, there was no one-to-one relationship between policy and power; an executive constitutionally enfeebled in its pursuit of one unpopular or unwise line of policy would be enfeebled in pursuing *any* line; a Congress stripped by the President of its consensual rights in one instance might be stripped with respect to all. During the Vietnam War, the struggle over policy came to be seen as one between a belligerent executive and a dovish Congress—as was also the case in pre-Pearl Harbor America. Yet the roles could be reversed easily, as may be seen on the eve of the Spanish-American War, when a hawkish Congress forced the reluctant McKinley administration to war. Another instance is to be seen in the period before the War of 1812, in which at one point in time Congress came near to declaring war on *both* Britain and Napoleonic France—a novel hypothetical circumstance, since these powers then were at war with each other. The Constitution does not specify which branch of government is a hawk and which a dove—neither, for that matter, whether the government or the public is. The broad, pathological anticommunism that suffused the American public during the Stalin-McCarthy period was not shared by the Truman administration.

The remark of John Locke in his *Civil Government* remained still applicable to the framing of the Constitution: The foreign-policy power, "in the well or ill management of it," necessarily had to be left "to the prudence and wisdom of those whose hands it is in, to be managed for the public good." A functional derangement of powers would affect not just one but all ranges of policy choices, and the nation would be rendered incapable of any purposeful and orchestrated action.

REVIEW QUESTIONS

1. How does the separation-of-powers doctrine relate to the asserted need for "secrecy and despatch" in the conduct of foreign affairs?

2. Are the powers of the Presidency in foreign affairs excessive? What might be the ways in which they could be limited? What might be the consequences of such limitations?

3. What problems occur for constitutional democracies in their adversary relations with totalitarian states?

4. How ought the "war-making" and "war-declaratory" powers of government be shared among branches of the federal government?

4 ON NATIONAL POWER

National power is political power possessed and deployable by a nation in dealings in a political environment that includes adversaries, friends, and others. It sometimes entails military operations or the threat of them; but war is only one manifestation of it, and an infrequent one at that. Much more important is the management of such power in such manner as to protect and advance interests and to deflect the occasions when war, especially general war, might otherwise erupt.

Power and the possession of it are essentially neutral from any ethical standpoint. The word "power" is derived through Old French from Latin origins that reveal its significance: *posse, potesse* connote "to be able," "to have power." Thus it is akin to other English words such as "potent," "potency," "potentiality," and "possible." The word thus signifies and combines purpose, ability, and possibility.

"Impotence" is the antonym of both "potency" and "power." Lord Acton, the British writer, in a regrettable aphorism, noted that "power tends to corrupt" and therefore that "absolute power corrupts absolutely." But the foolishness of this can be seen in its logical opposite, that is, if all impotence purifies, absolute impotence purifies absolutely. All forms of power are neutral or ambivalent, with respect to the possibilities of their use. This would be true even with respect to the most dramatic form of power harnessed by twentieth-century man, that of nuclear energy. Developed for military purposes, it soon was found also to have broad peaceful uses as well. The Wright brothers and Henry Ford welcomed the development of the airplane as an instrumentality of peace, since, facilitating contacts among men, it would improve international understanding. But military men quickly perceived it as a possible military weapon.

Political power is often chiefly defined as power *over* men (or over nations), which suggests a necessary hegemonic nature. As physical power connotes mastery over natural things, so political power is sometimes seen as mastery over men. Harold Lasswell's definition of political power, as that which determines "who gets what, where, when, why, and how," implies a distributive definition more akin to economics than to politics. Yet a moment's reflection suffices to show that power also may have as its object the freeing of men or the preserving of their freedom.

In any event, power has no meaning unless it is related to knowable ends. For such is the general nature of power that it can be manifest only in the real or purposed consequences of its use in concrete or hypothetical circumstances. Even in latent form, power is "power to," not simply "power." As the objects of our will can be many and different, so also the forms of power needed to attain them must differ; and, as should be self-evident, a specific form of power, by its very nature, in relation to some particular object may prove useless. A weight lifter has great power *to lift weights;* but his particular muscular strength would not make him a speedy 50-yard dash runner; it might, in fact, slow him considerably.

Power also must be seen in its proportional relationship to a specific object or end; for, as one could not likely have defeated a Hitler by employing mild, stubborn Gandhian tactics against him, so also one would not use hydrogen bombs for the deterrence or apprehension of speeding motorists. In the early days of the era of nuclear weapons, some referred to them as "absolute" weapons; however, in point of fact they proved otherwise, if only because of the proportional difficulty of relating them to finite political objects. There is, in fact, no absolute weapon or absolute multipurpose form of power, if the absoluteness refers to rational and positive purposes.

Omnipotence signifies the ability to obtain *any* ends whatsoever; "multipotence" (were there such an awkward word) can have operational meaning only when we are aware of the various kinds of objects or ends to which its components could be directed.

For these reasons, the idea of national power, conceived as uniting many qualities and quantities, tells us little about their pertinence as a whole to particular objects of statecraft. National power, considered as an agglomeration of quantifiable elements, is a murky conglomerate— which some who have dealt with it would see as a measurable combination of such factors as population, industrial and agricultural productivity, natural resources, skills, and technology. Weighing these factors and comparing them with similar qualities possessed by other states tell us little of their potency unless we speculate about the objects to which they might, in some coordinated fashion, be applied, and unless we consider also the *will* that can inform and guide them in certain directions. Thus it is that a willful state, with meager resources yet determined on the attainment of some specific end, may in this respect possess a greater influence over particular events than a far more richly endowed nation that is absorbed in many problems or is less resolute. Therefore, we often may be deceived about the actual power of a nation, if we observe merely the immensity of its resources, while neglecting the ends to which they are being put or ignoring the element of will and the strength of purpose that may actually exist in that nation and in its adversaries.

INFLUENCE AND FORCE

Considered as a purposed means to knowable ends, national power should be seen in two guises—influence and force. We might generally define *influence* as the ability to induce other people to do what we wish them to do; while *force* consists in making people do what they do not want to do (or, as deterrence theory suggests, in persuading them *not* to do what they would otherwise wish to do). Violent force is only one aspect of force—namely, force actually employed in destructive ways. Force may coerce in constructive directions; but violent force, by definition, is not in itself constructive.

Violent and constructive force, however, sometimes purposefully combine; and thus violence cannot always be deplored unless or until one considers its relationship to positive aims. Violence indulged in as an end in itself, violence purposefully exerted toward some obviously unattainable object, or violence used in a measure vastly in excess of its object ("overkill") all are morally repugnant.

In pursuit of particular ends of policy in international affairs, a nation often may employ its influence so as to reduce the likelihood of war, among others or between itself and others, and, paradoxically, may manipulate force so that violence will be less likely to occur. This is a perfectly justifiable end of statecraft. In the Middle East, for instance, American diplomacy since the 1950s has sought an arms equilibrium between Israel and the Arab states. To that end, the United States has given military aid to Israel, since a significant imbalance in strength might prove the occasion either for an Israeli preemptive strike (such as actually occurred in 1967) or for an Arab onslaught to destroy the state of Israel. Most states most of the time prefer to gain their ends without using destructive force; but even in such instances, influence is enhanced by the known existence of means of possible coercion, which lurk in the background—they may never be used, yet always they are sensed and appreciated. The possession of means of coercion, as well as means of rewards, enters into ratios of bargaining influence among nations even though there may be no immediate intention on anyone's part to employ them. Thus we have the peculiar Janus-headed nature of power-as-force in international politics: Its existence may serve the purpose of deterring and thus avoiding war, while its specific nature is always warlike. A military force created in a belief that its deterrent function would be so absolute as to wholly preclude the unpleasant possibility of its use would be a strange institution indeed—for its very credibility depends on its clear utility.

THE POWER OVER WAR AND PEACE

Students of international politics have long disputed the relationship between power and war and that between power and peace. In a general sense, some have argued a causal relationship between a state's acquisition and possession of means of violence and ensuing war. Arms races and the existence of armies and weapons have been regarded as the main, proximate causes of conflict; and the reverse is also said to be true, that is, disarmament or lowering of force levels may be antecedent to peace or the means by which international tensions can be lowered.

Yet there is another argument to the effect that the possession of means of force may deter acts of violence and war, if these means are in the hands of those who wish to keep the peace. If the price of provoking war can be set very high to those with aggressive designs, prudent behavior will be induced in those who otherwise would be tempted to use force were the price quite low. By analogy, consider the domestic role of the police with respect to the security of the community. Few would seriously argue that the existence of police or the production of small arms for police is a principal cause of crime. The chief strategic *raison d'être* of the police in normal circumstances is the deterrence of crime, not punishment of or combat with criminals.

There are flaws in both of these abstract sets of arguments. The mere absence of military power, as manifest in armies and navies, for example, is no guarantor of peace or promoter of "understanding" among nations. In 1860, for instance, on the eve of America's most horrible war, both North and South had little more than token military forces. Yet when war came, great military means for it were quickly found by both sides. In the 1930s, the reluctance of Western democracies to prepare themselves simply spurred Hitler's ambitions against the European order. Ironically, then, the "peace forces" inside the democracies, who prophetically pointed out the hideous character and consequences of war and the alleged profits of war to various economic groups, gravely weakened the will of the status-quo powers to take effective action until it was too late, until no options existed other than surrender or—paradoxically—the very total war they most had feared. Hesitant and unwilling to exert the deterrent influence of military force, the democracies were finally compelled to lavishly employ destructive power when both their efforts at conciliation and their deterrence had failed. The flaw in the "disarmament" position lies in its assumption that the possession of force must lead, inexorably, to its use; force long withheld, in the interest of conciliation, *in extremis* may have to be applied in far greater amounts than would have been needed at an earlier point in time.

The flaw in the second argument is that, in abstract, it cannot account for the fact that arms races, and the reciprocal fears that they often entail, in themselves can come to constitute a major source of tension between states, and military considerations can come to dominate political ones. Tension—if tension can be defined as an alert and fearful watchfulness reciprocated—is not in itself to be regarded as a condition necessarily antecedent to conflicts; conflicts often arise, paradoxically, under conditions in which reciprocated tensions did not precede them or at least did not play a prominent role in the circumstances leading to war.

An important instance of this is to be seen in the events immediately before the Russo-German war of 1941 to 1945. It was an object of Russian policy, before Hitler's attack, to avoid any appearance of hostility and to scrupulously comply with existing agreements with Hitler; and thus, Hitler, when preparing his savage attack, was spared the fulminating wrath that the Kremlin later lavished upon the Western democracies, when they protested and sought to control *Russian* expansion. Thus, deliberate calculated plans to launch aggressive war may not have antecedent and obvious phases of accelerated tension. During the cold war, the verbal abuse employed by Communist regimes against their adversaries often was correctly seen by influential Western statesmen as substitute for overt violence, rather than as preliminary indication of aggressive military plans. Yet it is certainly true that the fears generated by military-technological breakthroughs by one or another power may autonomously come to transcend the specific issues of political contention that at first may have given rise to them. Thus, arms races may, as it were, preempt the political arena. The main risk entailed in pursuing a strategy of rapidly acquiring military power, then, is the difficult one of trying to guess in advance its most likely effects upon the perceptions and calculations of adversaries. In the early 1950s, for instance, leaders of the Truman administration mistakenly believed that an American build-up of strength, commenced during the Korean War, would in consequence make Russian leaders more amenable to serious negotiations about important issues *for that reason*. What was left out of that calculation was the potential of the Soviet Union itself to respond by equally impressive increases in its already swollen military outlays. What is entailed in this question of the propriety of pushing military capabilities upward is a most difficult political calculation: In statecraft, the timing of policies and gestures with respect to situations rather than operating from abstract doctrines is crucial. Thus, a flaw in some conflict theories is to be seen in their abstract attempt to impose one or another doctrine on specific cases without first looking at the concrete uniqueness entailed in each. Charles Osgood's famous theory (of unilateral concessions in crisis situations, advocated on grounds that such acts would lead an adversary to reciprocate) overlooks the possibility that such concessions might be misinterpreted as weakness, not as conciliatory generosity. So also with Thomas Schelling's famous set of theories (derived from game theory and economics) that postulate conflict as a bargaining process; when applied to Vietnam, it overlooked the unpleasant possibility that—as far as the North Vietnamese were concerned—there was really nothing they wished to bargain over other than the modalities of their victory. Thus, calculated attempts to employ force with an object of exerting bargaining influence did not work in this instance. It is not that theory is irrelevant, but that theory, misapplied, can be catastrophic. In Vietnam, as Sir Robert Thompson observed, the fatal flaw of United States military policy lay in its search for military defeat of the enemy in the field, rather than in the construction of a viable political-military order in South Vietnam.

With respect, also, to the uses of military build-ups as means of being more "respected" as a power, there is the example of the fatal error in imperial German naval policy before World War I. The German government assumed that a massive fleet-building program would make Great Britain more respectful toward Germany and its interests; but precisely the opposite occurred; British anger and fears then became coupled with their lack of confidence in Germany. The two nations moved into stances of rivalry that proved disastrous later to Germany, if not to both.

POWER AS A RESOURCE AMALGAM

National power, comprehending but certainly not confined to military force, represents at any time a combination of various elements; these are tangible and intangible, measurable and unmeasurable, latent and manifest. An ideal, yet potentially pernicious, view would be to see national power as an architectonic, orchestrated whole, in which parts are linked harmoniously in the pursuit of some known national goals. In such fashion, it would be seen as the totality of a nation, comprising its population, natural resources, industrial plant, productivity, and technical know-how; its military forces; its administrative and diplomatic skills; its moral, social cohesiveness; and so forth. Great powers are reputed to have many of these in abundance. In today's Balkanized world, there are only a few of them. Such qualities are not necessarily more desirable than the attributes of smaller, less influential, yet pleasant countries. However, the plenitude of human and material resources, the wide span of potential effective influence, and a reputation of actually *being* powerful and legitimate distinguish the great power from others—this says nothing as to the wisdom or morality of its courses of action but much as to what effects it can have upon others and on the attainment of ends, simply by "being" powerful.

The nature of a so-called great power is such that whether it wishes or not, other nations depend upon and may be greatly affected by its actions or inactions. In alliance-coalitions, a leading power, such as the United States today, while it may not willfully or intentionally neglect its own interests, nevertheless cannot afford to ignore or repudiate the "general welfare" of the aggregation of states of which it is a part. This was illustrated in July 1971, when President Nixon, in announcing his astounding decision to visit Peking, assured the world that this decision in no way affected America's commitments to its friends, nor was it directed against any other nation. The reassurance was by no means wholly reassuring, but it also was not hypocritical, for the loss of confidence among friends would be a severe price to pay for seeking a problematic accommodation with an adversary.

The span and nature of the influence of a great power, however, may sometimes not be a matter of deliberate and national choice but rather, at times, simply the consequence of its very existence and of historical circumstance. While America as a power pursued its political policy of isolationism through the first months of World War II, allying itself with no other state and confining its stated interests principally to the Western Hemisphere, there was at the time absolutely no doubt that its collective influence on events in other parts of the world was very great indeed—this, although the sum total of its multifarious activities might have represented no distinct or contrived purpose, and added up to none. Some American diplomatic historians have not helped to clarify this paradoxical aspect of great-power behavior, that the nation may influence and affect without a strategic purpose. William Appleman Williams, for instance, conscious of the important effects exerted by America's civilization in both Asia and Europe, was for this reason moved to describe American isolationism as a "myth," covering up an energetic, expansionist process. In this, he is wholly mistaken, if we are to define isolationism in American history as a posture and policy of willfully refusing to act with others in concert or alliance for purposes of national security. While the American economy exerted important effects (many of these unintended) on the world economy before 1939, it was the deliberate withholding of American political influence over the affairs of Europe that had such negative and severe consequences. However imperialistic, no calculated foreign policy of expansion successfully could be sustained in disregard of the needs for calculated political policies to protect it; the American refusal to acknowledge this fact came rather belatedly. See Williams' *Tragedy of American Diplomacy*.[1] Left critics of American diplomatic history, typically, also ignore real security problems faced by the American nation, while characteristically exaggerating American threats to others.

EFFECTS OF TIME UPON POWER

Time bears crucially upon the nature of power, as can be seen when we commonly distinguish between "power" and "potential" in ordinary usage. What is "potential" is some latent yet discernible talent or strength not now manifest or readily available, while the notion of power is that of a quality already in being or usable. There is a distinction between latent power (a potentiality) and power-in-being. The latent power of a nation lies in what it later may be able to develop and apply to circumstances, yet cannot now apply. By analogy, the potentiality of a young pianist may be elicited and trained so that he might become a great musician, but potentiality alone will not suffice to put him right away on the stage in Carnegie Hall or the Lincoln Center.

In relation to its bearing upon concrete circumstances and policy questions, *latent* power must be considered differently from power-in-being. Here, the likely time span between the date at which a potentiality

---

[1] William Appleman Williams, *The Tragedy of American Diplomacy,* Dell Publishing Co., Inc., New York, 1962.

begins to be nurtured and the time at which it might be manifest and applied is of great importance. For a potentiality is of no use if on an occasion of its need it is not so actualized as to be applied. In 1940, a desperate premier of France appealed to America to send "clouds of planes" to assist his collapsing armies; but even if the Roosevelt administration then had been sympathetic to the plea, there were no such clouds-in-being. Three years later, American aircraft production reached levels of production (100,000 per year) that in 1940 had been unthinkable to all but a few production specialists. But by then of course the original occasion had long since passed; the European continent was overridden by German armies, and vast sacrifices and destruction proved necessary to regain what much less, previously, could have held. The potentiality had been there in 1940, not the actuality.

Today, the problem of latent power is especially acute in questions of national security, with respect to the time necessary not simply to produce quantities of instrumentalities, but to actually develop their nature and forms. The problem for the distressed French premier in 1940 was to obtain quantities of a weapon (aircraft) the nature and form of which already existed in inadequate numbers. The problem that later acutely came to affect considerations of national security was that of the "lead time" in developing qualitatively new types of weaponry in fluid technological circumstances. In this, the time span between initial research and development and actual deployment may range between 5 and 15 years, depending upon complexity and rapidity of new developments requiring changes or redesigning. The problem thus is not merely the actualization of potentialities but also the "potentializing of potentialities." The withering of research and development, in circumstances of current strategic equilibrium in relations among powers, might not effect a strategic balance until years later; then the effect might be very pronounced. This is so, because of the continuing speed of technological innovations. For instance, in lead time, the Soviet Union in 1970 well may have been far ahead of the United States in developing and even deploying *mobile* ICBM capabilities.[2] Thus power must be seen in these dimensions of time.

[2] Testimony of Dr. John S. Foster, Director of Defense Research and Engineering, before subcommittee of the House Armed Services Committee, 91st Cong., 2d Sess., Mar. 9, 1970, p. 12.

In the history of American foreign relations, with respect to this matter of potentiality and actuality in the power equation of the nation, a harsh dividing line may be drawn between two sets of historical circumstances: that which, generally speaking, prevailed before 1939, and that which subsequently has obtained, and which—so it would seem—appears as a permanent condition. In the "traditional" American condition in world politics before World War II, time and space served as buffers between the nation and significant external threats to its security. Together, they permitted a relatively leisurely and considered response to serious crises in those world "power zones" that have been the chief sources of external danger to American security. In the derangements of the European order during the Napoleonic Wars, nine years elapsed between the commencement of Europe's most serious derangement of equilibrium and the time when American power came to play an effective part in the disturbances. In those of World War I, nearly three years elapsed. In World War II, also, nearly three years elapsed between Hitler's invasion of Poland and the Japanese attack on Pearl Harbor. One might have argued the desirability of American power being applied earlier in both previous circumstances; yet it was not absolutely necessary, to American survival, that that be the case.

So it was that in the pre-1939 phase of American foreign relations, this time-space buffer made it possible for a nation in peace to rely for its protection upon its latent capabilities and for that nation in times of war to make preparations, to mobilize and employ them, and, following war, to demobilize them in such a way that they were returned to their "original" peacetime functions, which were considered to be the norm. This was true even after World War II; within a two-year period between 1945 and 1947, the United States military establishment (other than the Navy and the Strategic Air Command) was pared to the bone, and acute pressure was exerted on the Truman administration, through Congress, to quickly eliminate all remaining wartime controls on wages, prices, and production.

This process of reconversion bespoke a traditional American habit of regarding wartime as an acute, abnormal phase of national life that, when passed through, could be regarded as "over," whereupon the agencies that war required could be drastically reduced in their proportions or even eliminated. So also, emergency wartime powers of the Presidency, swollen by crises, could be pared back and curtailed. In a long time span, embracing not only war and peace, but the intervening time spaces, we may then generally distinguish a classical American time cycle with respect to power: war → postwar demobilization → "normalcy" → perceived impending crisis → prewar mobilization. Of these phases, that of "normalcy" was perceived to be the norm; and this, historically, has been true: Of the 150 years of America's history as an independent nation before 1939, in only 10 was actual war being officially waged. In peacetime, the resources of the nation were employed in peaceful uses of a consumer-oriented economy. "Power," conceived of as instrumentality of security, lay encapsulated as "potentiality" in the ongoing and diffuse activities of an open society.

The shrinkage of time and space—a process slowly under way in the centuries before World War II—was vastly accelerated in the years that immediately followed. Distance—the space between one object or place and another—must be known in its several aspects, among which, measurable physical distance (e.g., miles, kilometers) is only an artificial contrivance. We may speak, for instance, of distance in terms of *cost* of transferring or transporting or of the *time* entailed in transfer or contact or of contrived or natural *impediments* to such contact or movement. The illusion of distance today is principally cartographical; for as a physically close person may be said to be "unapproachable" or "distant," so also a cartographically remote person or nation may seem quite "close." From a *cost* point of view—namely, relative cost factors pertaining to shifting of supplies and people—South Vietnam (as Albert Wohlstetter has pointed out) is "closer" to the East Coast of the United States, than (for instance) to China. In premodern times, a whole decade could elapse while a communication was sent from one part of the world to another. Marco Polo, for instance, tells the story of the magnificent sea expedition fitted out and sent by the court of the Great Khan to bring a new tribal princess to the court of one of his Persian vassals, to be his new wife; the splendid retinue arrived, only to discover that the king, and the putative consort, had died years before. Yet this impediment of physical space can be seen in a more recent story: Immediately after the attack on Pearl Harbor on December 7, 1941, the then Secretary of the Navy, Frank Knox, and a retinue were dispatched to Hawaii by airplane on urgent mission to survey the extent of damage to the American fleet; this hasty expedition from Washington, to what is now one state of the Union, took more than one week. It took President Franklin D. Roosevelt more than 15 days, in early 1945, to travel to the Crimea for his wartime conference with Churchill and Stalin.

The shrinkage of distance in the years following World War II was evidenced most dramatically in the collapse of "strategic distance," if by this we mean the proximity of potentially hostile, or really hostile, power. In 1940, an American President, seeking to alert the American public to the danger posed by German domination of Europe, attempted with limited success to point out the proximity of this power to America and the Western Hemisphere and the implications of this proximity, should the British buffer separating it from North America be removed. At that time, however, the argument thesis of vulnerability was questionable: Given the then-existing technology of war, it was questionable whether Nazi air, naval, or land power could seriously have affected the security of continental America. This condition, however, which had served as a buffer for American defense, providing both time and space for protection, no longer exists as far as strategic weapons go; in this respect, no part of the North American continent is more than a few minutes removed from possible hostile attack by the worst of all weapons. Since the Soviets' acquisition of ICBMs in the late 1950s, this brink of catastrophe has become the "normal" condition for American security, or, rather, insecurity; and it is, in theory at least, "normal" for every nation in the world. The obliteration of time and space with respect to *attack* weaponry thus has severely altered the kinds of conditions under which decisions of war and peace might be made. The classic separation of powers relative to foreign affairs, framed to check and distribute authority over the making of treaties, the formal commencement and ending of war, the conduct of diplomacy, and the conduct of military operations, has been profoundly affected by this.

So also, this shrinkage of time and space has caused a radical change in the relationship between latent and manifest power. For where American defense classically reposed in the idea of the "Minuteman," the peaceable citizen with his peaceable economy who in time of crisis could convert self and resources to martial purposes, the security problem in the thermonuclear era could no longer be met in that fashion. Ironically, while today's Minuteman missiles, installed in immense bunkers, serve the peace as deterrents to attack, they have no other civic use and thus contradict the classic symbolism of their name. For certain hypothetical kinds of conflict, forces-in-being were the only ones that could be regarded as effective; and thus, after 1950, the American military establishment remained on a high footing of readiness, with huge annual budgetary appropriations, accounting for nearly 7 percent of the American gross national product. In this respect, the alertness of military force for deterrent purposes had effectively eliminated the classic stages of American posture; as an English historian put it, the new condition was that of "no peace, no war."

THE RELATION OF POWER TO OTHER POWER

Finally, power is relational: it bears not simply upon some object or purpose, but on how the power a nation possesses relates to that which others possess. Such comparisons are not necessarily adversary evaluations; power being respected in the calculations of states, it is taken into account by all, adversaries, friends, and others, in judging the relationships that are affected by it. For this reason, even in the absence of current hostilities among states or even of great tensions among them, such comparisons invariably are made. In the American instance, in the period after World War II, this came down to its reputation as a superpower—a reputation that was an agglomerate of many elements of reputation: its enormous gross national productivity, and the surplus from this GNP that could be tapped for aid and assistance to others; its military establishment, which after 1945 included atomic weapons but which by 1945 had grown to be the most versatile, mobile combination of elements that the world had heretofore seen. The American reputation as superpower consisted also in the sudden sway that it came to exert over the world economy—an economy that had been gravely damaged and reduced by the war and had lost its traditional moorings and dependence upon the British Empire. The growth of this American power to superpower status should not be accounted for in absolute terms; while it was true that the American economy made stupendous strides in productivity during the four years of United States wartime involvement, this alone could not account for the enormous qualitative changes that subsequently became apparent when the dust had settled. Rather, in relative terms what occurred between 1939 and 1945 was the collapse of nearly all the classic powers in war, the enormous reduction in British resources and capabilities, and the vast destruction wrought on the

Soviet Union. It is therefore little wonder that for more than a decade after that war, the United States was able itself to initiate a vast range of changes in the scenery of international relations, not simply on behalf of its own specific national interests, but also in order to create a new system of relations, which, in absence of American initiatives and designs, would have taken far longer to emerge and would have been of an entirely different character. Thus, between 1945 and 1955, the resources of American power were put behind the *establishment* of a new order of international things, rather than behind the maintenance of something older, which in any event did not exist. (It is probably for this reason that former Secretary of State Dean Acheson, active in the Roosevelt and Truman administrations when these changes were effected, immodestly titled his autobiographical account of those years *Present at the Creation.*)

Invariably, when a historic opportunity of this sort arises for a state, while its actions may transcend its classical conceptions of national interests, its conception of supranational designs are heavily influenced by its own national conceptions. During these formative years of the postwar international system, specifically American contours came to inform the nature of the relations and the content of the institutions that established the uniqueness of the postwar period. Thus, the incessant American pressure upon allies and neutrals alike brought into being in 1945 the United Nations organization and crucially affected the shape of that institution—as in fact had been the case after World War I. Thus also, in the designing of a postwar format of international economic systems, the American stress upon liberal trade policies and rejection of nationalist, particularist protective policies, set the seal upon the dominant trading world. In this instance, the firm and even dogmatic American assumption was that protective trade barriers and exclusionary bargaining practices in international monetary policy had been among the principal causes of the rivalries of states that led to World War II. It is especially necessary for us to see, in the designing of international monetary institutions, the reflection of an important fact: The new international monetary standard that emerged after the war was the American dollar. All currencies were measured by it; and in this sense it became surrogate for the international gold standard that had been generally accepted during the great universalist period of peace during the nineteenth century. Finally, the various alliance systems that the

United States forged and joined gave new shape to the international system as adjunct to the United Nations universalist system that preceded them. In all these developments, again, it is necessary to see that the American innovative role was ascribable, not simply to its increased, augmented absolute strength, but rather to the relation of this strength to the general chaos that surrounded it and that American policy had not been directed to attain that innovative role.

For several years after World War II, many Americans like others, misjudged the extent to which the older order of things in world politics had actually been mortally weakened. During the war and immediately afterward, many Americans—Roosevelt included—had tended to assume mistakenly that the principal rivalry of the United States would be with Great Britain, over trade policy, self-determination for colonial possessions, and policy in Europe. Roosevelt, at the Yalta Conference with Churchill and Stalin, fancied himself in the role of mediator between the British Empire and the Soviet Union, a role that Stalin was quick to encourage since it divided the two on such crucial questions as Poland and policy toward the other Eastern European countries. Yet this anticipated rivalry never matured; and precisely the opposite occurred, when it became evident that Britain, its resources bled dry in the war, was in no position long to retain its empire or its strategic "responsibilities," which classically it had carried out in much of the non-European world since the time of Napoleon. This structural collapse, which followed fast on the heels of the collapse of the continental European states, contributed far more to the enlargement of American "spheres of influence" than any deliberate United States policy decisions that accompanied it and that in any event tended to be improvised rather than calculated. Thus, in 1947, the American decision to fill British shoes in Greece was seen by few for what it really portended; namely, that the United States would become the major Mediterranean naval power and would acquire strategic interests that, traditionally, some Western power exercised in the Eastern Mediterranean and the Middle East. Such were the systemic changes of that time and such was the speed with which they arose, that United States policy makers often, in responding to them, assumed that American responses were going to be only transitory and even self-liquidating rather than permanent.

After the fact, some came to call the new structure of relationships outside the Communist world (which remained a thing apart) the *Pax*

Americana, as though the achieved normalcy that finally became manifest 15 years after the end of World War II were a residuary legacy of the *Pax Britannica,* the relatively tranquil condition of political stability in the extra-European world that historians attribute to the naval supremacy of Great Britain until 1914. Within this framework of political relationships, sustained by an American alliance system, regularities and predictabilities of human life that could exist within such a calculus of normality could apply. Under the *Pax Britannica,* British power had not been everywhere applied, nor had the world been subjugated by British control; rather, where British power could touch or where it could insulate situations from the rivalry of other major states, major international conflicts had been deterred or prevented; likewise, British financial and economic systems, being the dominant regulatory institutions that this world responded to, provided a sense of predictability and order within which economic development could and did occur.

In two respects, however, what came to pass as a *Pax Americana* differed sharply from its nineteenth-century predecessor. For one thing, the British system of naval supremacy had coincided with or overlapped the period of Britain's major imperial colonization, which to some extent was informed by an imperial ethic of the "white man's burden." The *Pax Americana,* if we can call it that, explicitly rejected the idea of colonization and direct control, and in fact—in its general rejection of colonialism—hastened the process of liquidation of the great European empires.

It is interesting that the one instance—Indochina—in which postwar American policy, for complex reasons, chose instead to support European (French) colonialism, proved to be the occasion of America's most disillusioning war. Basically, in that instance, two considerations pushed American policy in that direction: first, tough French insistence, in 1953, for such support as condition for its effective participation in European defense; second, a fear of peripheral Communist Chinese expansion in Southeast Asia. In virtually all other instances, it was American policy in the 1950s and 1960s to support independence for colonial peoples; and it is not uninteresting that one of the great Third World revolutionary theoreticians, Franz Fanon, died in Washington, D.C. It is beside the point to ask whether this process of decolonization proceeded too quickly; the point being that in most instances the pace of it was quickened by United States support of it. The notable lack of strong public support of United States involvement in the Vietnam War could be attributed, if incorrectly, to strong American animus against colonialism, even if practiced by the United States.

We could also distinguish the so-called *Pax Americana* from its nineteenth-century forebear, by pointing out that they differed in one crucial strategic respect. It was British policy, after the Napoleonic Wars, indirectly to nourish an equilibrium among the other great powers of Europe, so that no one of them alone would dominate the European continent and so that, with all of them sensitive to the delicacy of that balance, none would seriously challenge British command of the seas to undertake overseas expansion that might create for Britain a global rival. (Thus it was that Britain in the 1820s warned both France and the Holy Alliance from taking measures to preserve the Spanish colonies in the Western Hemisphere by force.) Save in special instances, this British policy did not entail serious direct involvement in the power politics of the European mainland, which continued to be the cockpit of world politics. There, the sustained equilibrium of Continental power served to negate the exercise of that power elsewhere; and the *Pax Britannica,* relying upon that condition, was able elsewhere to obtain its objects with an economy of power.

In the post-World War II period, however, American power after 1945 was exerted directly and continually in both Europe and the world outside of it: United States ground forces and strategic air power in Europe after 1950 in a sense became local hostages to a new counter-poise to the Soviet Union, one which, in their absence, would not have lasted long. Thus this new *Pax Americana,* like the *Pax Britannica* of the nineteenth century, deemed the European continent to be the central seat of a test of equilibrium, yet direct American presence in the situation of encounter was a close, intimate one. The relationship of the United States to its allies here was of necessity a hegemonial one when it came to questions of strategic power. Underneath that clear hegemony, however, Western European political developments followed their own momentum and their own purposes. The American relationship of power became like an umbrella, deterring Soviet aims to dominate Europe, yet not determining the internal processes of European politics. In this instance, a consensus, spelled out only partly in the North Atlantic Treaty, lay between the United States and its European allies, joining their effective military forces and their policies to deter further Soviet pressures westward. The Soviet position in Eastern Europe, extending into central Germany, continued to constitute a threat to the security of Western Europe, while Soviet diplomacy had as principal object the withdrawal of American power from Europe and the latter's neutralization or capitulation.

VARYING THE INGREDIENTS OF POWER

National power, as we have seen, means more than a diffuse "influence," in that it aims for desired goals, which might be achieved regardless of other states' attitudes. It also means more than force, which is simply one aspect of power and is used by most nations only reluctantly; and much more than destructive force, that which destroys in order to achieve ends. A crucial test of statecraft is to find the ways in which nondestructive and creative forms of power may gain ends that coercion and destructive force might also seek. At the same time, it must also recognize the unpleasant occasions in which there is no adequate substitute for force and still other circumstances in which a mixture of rewards and threats might obtain goals that could not be achieved by one or the other exerted separately. In history, no state has long survived or prospered that relied solely on force or solely on good will, benign gestures, or rewards as central elements in its foreign policies. In American foreign policy, a particular success story or a particular failure story with respect to the application of a mixture of force and generosity may be deceptive for later uses.

The story of the American Marshall Plan (1947 to 1951) in Europe importantly illustrates the point. In 1948, when the Soviet Union and the United States contested for the fate of Central and Western Europe, their means differed sharply. The assets (means) of the two sharply differed. In the American instance, influence was applied from a vast cornucopia of American economic bounty, both to reestablish war-torn European national economies and to prevent their domination by the Soviet Union. At that time, United States military forces had reached a low point of current effectiveness. (There were then only two combat-ready United States divisions on the European continent, for example.)

This leverage of influence served decisively to strengthen the democrat-ic forces of Western Europe and Germany, even while American military strength continued to decline (as it did, until the Korean War in 1950).

In the Russian instance, in the same period, an attempt to extend control westward in Europe and to augment the strength of the Soviet Union in other ways involved the application of different devices; here, influence was applied by means of force and deprivation. Torn by the destruction of the war, yet retaining much of its huge wartime military establishment, the Soviet Union—anxious to recover its own strength—stripped nations in its orbit of their means of productivity and absorbed and threatened others by its military power. This particular contest lay in the confrontation of two different strategies: in the American, a policy of rewards and incentives was uppermost; in the Russian, a policy of spoliation and force prevailed. Yet each policy reflected the peculiar assets of each contender; quite possibly, in this encounter, the Russians may have envied their affluent rivals the means that Americans were able to employ. Yet in the outcome, the American reputation was the more appreciated by its beneficiaries and was reflected in the successful outcome. (One interesting aspect of the encounter lay in the confronta-tion for control within France: when the French Communist Party, under orders from Moscow, sought beginning in 1947 to combat the United States Marshall Plan, its chief weapon was that of the strike—yet the strike itself hit at the most basic goal desired by most Frenchmen, that of economic recovery, and thus alienated the overwhelming numbers of Frenchmen who saw in recovery a principal value.)

It is clear from this instance that a strong admixture of economic assistance accomplished policy ends that, conceivably, force might also have obtained. However, it is important also to note that there are many circumstances in which this is not so. Attempts, for example, by Ameri-can policy makers in the Middle East to induce peaceful settlement between Arabs and Israelis through offers of great economic aid, thus far have failed in their object. For many Arabs, national liberation proved a more attractive object than prosperity or economic improvement; while, for Israelis, guaranteed military security is deemed more important than the prospect, for instance, of a fruitful cooperative economic develop-ment of the Jordan River valley. So also, in Vietnam, economic reform and offers of great programs of development, such as the Mekong River

Valley project, in no way deflected Vietnamese Communists from their political goal of dominating Indochina; while in the countryside, land reform proved to be a useless chimera as means to political stability while trained revolutionaries were able to terrorize and exterminate its immediate or potential beneficiaries. Quite often, in insurgency warfare, a strategy of economic deprivation confronts a strategy of economic reward, in the struggle to control disputed areas. Paradoxically, the former often proves more effective than the latter, since terror in specific circumstances more powerfully inspires cowardice, than reward spurs courage. This fundamental asymmetry in Vietnam never was appreciated by those Americans who saw in economic aid the principal weapon against Communist terror in winning allegiance of peasant communities—a perverse application of the Marshall Plan lesson in circumstances where it was bound to fail.

We see then from the above that power-as-influence cannot be prepared in advance, as a boxed cake mix, with its ingredients prescribed beforehand; for while in the baking of a cake, the cook commands meticulous control of the "environment" the ingredients occupy, it is in the nature of foreign-policy situations that the need to concoct new mixes of power and influence arises precisely because the environment seems likely to be getting out of control. Thus the uncertainty of circumstances makes the choice of mix crucial, yet complex and hazardous—especially so, since in all circumstances, responses to situations must improvise from readily accessible resources and skills, rather than from some ideal configuration of power that one might like to have.

The American improvisation of the airlift in the Berlin crisis of 1948 and 1949 enabled American policy makers to avoid the extreme choice between armed confrontation with the Russians and capitulation. Before it was contrived as an urban supply system, no one had ever imagined it as such; yet the existence of huge numbers of British and American transport planes made it feasible. A diversity of resources enables the policy maker to avoid the bleak circumstance of reliance on a single blunt device; and it might for that reason be an argument for national power, that this should comprise a panoply of capabilities, lest an overhoarding of one set of attitudes, responses, or techniques, prove useless in changed circumstances.

REVIEW QUESTIONS

1. What is the relationship of national power to national purpose and will? Are the latter to be regarded as ingredients of power or the guides to power?

2. Some people argue the utility of national force as means of keeping the peace; others argue that the acquisition of force leads to war. Are either of these views more than partial glimpses of the nature of power?

3. Discuss the difference between power-in-being and latent power. Can the latter exert any effects upon current circumstances?

4. While neither the United States nor the Soviet Union radically increased its national power in any absolute sense during World War II, they quickly became reputed as the two "superpowers" in the war's aftermath. Why was this so?

5 ON RELATIONSHIPS

To encourage a tolerable milieu for the United States after World War II, a central object of American policy was to encourage in East Asia and in Europe equilibriums of political power so that neither area would be dominated or threatened with domination by one indigenous state. So great were the derangements of political relationships during and after World War II, however, that this supreme object became involved with two structural conditions—an unforeseen fact of American-Russian bipolarity and an unforeseen fusion of ideological conflict with great-power rivalry. During most of the 1950s and 1960s, as a result of this fusion of power and ideology, in many basic respects international politics attained a popular appearance of majestic simplicity rare in the history of world politics. States and nations in alliance became dialectically polarized in tension with each other.

For their part, Soviet leaders described this as a "two-camp" division of the world between the so-called socialist bloc and that of the "capitalist world"; American leaders subsequently designated it as one between a free world and a totalitarian one. Alongside these two aggregations of power, many states in the newly independent world of Africa and Asia sought postures of nonalignment and neutralism. Rejecting close identification with either bloc, such states then sought to play conciliatory roles in this rivalry or to exploit it to their own national purposes. The rift of the power blocs was of great spatial dimension. The umbrellalike hegemony of the two giant powers covered most of the industrially developed world. Seeing the cold-war era as one of conflict and competition between these two blocs, we may in consequence fail to appreciate its "ordering" nature, namely, that the restructuring of world politics around the poles of Moscow and Washington followed and therefore replaced an authentic and very unstable era of international anarchy. In Europe, for instance, in the 1930s the map of international politics had resembled a calico bedspread; the absence of durable alliances and blocs made the international system much more resemble that of Hobbes's state of nature, than the cold-war bloc system did.

One main feature of the cold war thus was a pronounced tendency toward political integration on a scale never before known in history. This process sharply contrasted with an opposite tendency in the so-called Third World. As decolonization proceeded, political fragmentation occurred; and the new aspiration was toward autonomy, not integration. Old nationalist enmities—between France and Germany, for instance— were simply washed away by the new ordering of things, while, in areas under sway of Russian imperialism in Eastern Europe, vicious national rivalries were suppressed along with national freedoms. Paradoxically, the conflicts most destructive of human life, in peak years of the cold war, occurred either in geographic situations far removed from areas of most acute interest to the superpowers and their chief allies or in places where neither Moscow nor Washington successfully could subdue local rivalries. On the Indian subcontinent, in Indonesia, the Sudan, Nigeria, China, North Africa, and the Middle East—in such places, rather than where the superpowers directly confronted each other, scourges of civil and international war played themselves out without control of the major powers. But a peace of reciprocated, managed tension reigned in those central strategic areas where war and the instabilities that usually precede it were intolerable prospects for the nations that still knew the horrible realities from immediate past experience.[1]

As American strategic aims evolved in the cold war, an awkward tension arose between aspirations and pragmatic policies. American policy aspired to a new future shape of international equilibrium in which, as allies recovered old or attained new strength, American support of them could phase out or be qualitatively reduced. Thus, in Western Europe, one aspiration of American· policy was to seek, by way of economic and political integration, a new equipoise in which the burden of Western defense and the strategic balance would rest less onerously on American shoulders. However, the general direction of things is shaped by short-range tendencies, crises, necessities, and decisions, and realization of policy aspirations was not so simple. A basic day-to-day necessity lay in sustaining a European strategic balance. The structure of that balance on the Western side of it entailed the presence of American power. Europeans came to take this presence for granted, thus further institutionalizing it and deferring indefinitely the very measures of European strategic and political coordination that might have rendered American hegemony less crucial. At any time, a calculated American force reduction, if not reciprocated by the Soviet Union, might be mistaken by Europeans as sign of an American neoisolationism or might be taken as indication of some tacit American *détente* with Russia. In either case, the likely European responses were not promising. In the first instance, a fear of American abandonment might result in a steady slippage of Western Europe into a posture of passive neutralism vis-à-vis Russia, a posture sustained by no internal strength. While in the second instance, were Europe to imitate an American force reduction, this would lead also to much the same results. In such fashions, the central strategic object of American diplomacy in Europe would be lost.

[1] This is of course written with placid benefit of hindsight since the acute crises over Berlin, Cuba, and so forth, did not escalate into major war. Each of the postwar crises between the superpowers was a consequence of Soviet attempts forcibly to change the status quo. The point here is that great tension, in these central strategic areas, produced conditions of relative stability that uncontrolled political change would have threatened.

THE COLD-WAR SYSTEM AS SUBSTITUTE FOR ANARCHY

Considering that the cold war has been a time when great tension combined with extensive political order, we might examine some of its distinctive qualities more closely. While bipolarity contained frightening possibilities of general war, it also developed certain stabilizing features in the 1950s and 1960s. Many Americans, discontented at its contrary, frightening features, were less perceiving of its more benign ones. Yet clearly, the stabilities involved had greatly reduced the anarchic potential in international politics. Were one to address the question of what might replace the ordered condition of cold-war rivalry, he might commence by asking first what new national posture the United States might itself take toward the condition ("reexamining its commitments") or ask what substitute system of political relationships might sequentially be induced to replace it as something "better." The two questions could be seen as quite different. Since the United States was chiefly responsible for establishing the general architecture of postwar international politics (in the developed world at least), it remained an American option at all times to abandon this responsibility, reverting to a withdrawn posture and cutting its commitments. Or it could choose in calculated fashion to play a more flexible, opportunistic, yet quite active international role, having, in the words of Washington's Farewell Address, no permanent friends, no permanent adversaries, only duties and interests. Whichever option was taken, among the consequences of either policy would be new psychological uncertainties in the international situation—where it was moving, and what it portended.

While most people take their cues about the state of world politics from headlines and television, a severe price of this "existential" view of foreign policy is that its sensitivity to immediate facts and realities is befriended by a dulled awareness of many contingencies, possibilities, and future purposes. Likes and dislikes, fears and favoritisms, cluster around these immediate facts; and those immediate things one would wish to preserve or change, alter or destroy, become the only concrete and tangible objects of concern. Thus, through the latter years of the Vietnam War, American attitudes toward foreign policy became fused to one "immediate" experience, and much else in the meantime was ignored; popular concern focuses chiefly on the termination of a costly and frustrating experience.

But policy always must address itself to what is next to be done, rather than to what was or was not done in the past. It must have ampler dimensions than such an existential perspective supplies. In serious times of choice, paradoxically, the moods and the passions of indifference or excitement engendered by this existential view either paralyze policy or excessively endow it with the energy of needed public support.

One reason why history supplies no sure answers to policy choices in foreign affairs is that each generation remembers its own special history. Every cat (to borrow Mark Twain's adage again) may recall its own experience of pain on a particular hot stove; but the stoves marvelously differ in appearance and intensity of temperature. What one generation may seek strenuously to avoid, then, another may innocently have little or no knowledge of. What the American Depression was to one generation of Americans, pollution (a product of affluence, not misery) became to another; the skies of America were purer when half its industrial plant was closed and families starved. An older generation remembers the Depression, Munich, and real global war; a new one knows affluence (and its prices) and Vietnam.

History, however, is not simply remembered experience; it contains many experiences each of which conveys its own learning. In terms of international politics, a knowledge of various past structures of politics may help to indicate future possibilities, dangers, and opportunities. Since ours has been an era of the cold war, it might be useful to look back at circumstances that bear little structural resemblance to it, yet that very probably could resemble the immediate future of the international system.

THE TRANSIENCY OF IDEOLOGICAL EPOCHS

Only at certain times in past history, as now, have configurations of international relations been characterized by intense and extensive ideological warfare. More typical of international relations have been the long times in which conflict and cooperation among states have been determined by much less universalistic and philosophical considerations.

The wars and hostilities between Christendom and Moslems; between Catholic Europe and Protestant Europe; between Revolutionary France and the remainder of Europe; between Leninist Marxism of the communist world and the rest of humanity—such epochs are finite periods and between them "other things happen," usually less dramatically. These times of ideological supremacy have been of limited scope. They wane, giving way to newer and far more complicated circumstances. Even during them, there is an impurity and inexactitude in the polarization that they engender; thus, Christian France under Louis XIV collaborated with Ottoman Turks, whom many Europeans felt to be the enemies of the faith; during the wars of Catholic and Protestant Europe, Gustavus Adolphus of Protestant Sweden collaborated with Catholic France in wars in Central Europe against the Hapsburgs. So also in the cold war; the imperfections in ideological polarization were to be seen in Communist Yugoslavia's special relation to democratic, "capitalist" America, and in Franco Spain's relationship to Castro's Cuba. Total polarization never occurred.

When universal ideologies wane, they disjoint themselves from considerations of state power; foreign policy, cut loose from "belief," becomes exceptionally complex and fluid. When a calculus of belief gives way to one of interest, the cement of universalism cracks and can disintegrate. Now, there are not "two" sides, but many independent national actors, each consulting its own interests. For example, in Europe after the Napoleonic Wars a multiple balance among many states came to be regarded as a normal configuration in international life. The possibilities of conflict and cooperation were rich in prospects of combinations. The modes of interaction among the principal states of Europe—such as Britain, France, Russia, Imperial Germany—then had little to do with the special distinctive social systems of any of them or with their belief structures and ideologies; but the interaction modes did have a great deal to do with nationalism. Thus in the last part of the nineteenth century and the first half of the twentieth, particularistic nationalism and national rivalries were the principal sources of hostilities in world politics, while the universalistic pretensions and promises of Marxism and American liberalism both merely preached panaceas of future harmony. (In 1918, it should be remembered, both Lenin and Wilson each in his own way offered systematic panaceas for the defects in an old order with which neither had had any experience.)

One disconcerting aspect of international equilibrium, as Hedley Bull has observed, is that such equilibrium depends on the existence of a certain tension and conflict among great powers. Equilibrium thus can be threatened in some situations by understandings arrived at by great powers that lessen their animosity to each other in specific circumstances.[2] This is so, because the lessening of such animosity often is purchased at the expense of the interests of other states. Thus, an accommodation between America and China could carry grave implications for the future of Taiwan and could set in motion chains of possible events adverse to Communist China's other adversaries.

Tension among great powers is never abstract; it clusters around specific objects. Frequently, these are matters of most special concern to other states. As long as there exists a fixity of relations among alliance partners, in clearly delinable patterns, there exists of course the risk that large conflict between blocs may arise from specific things; yet the danger that inheres in *détente* lies in the transitional, uncertain process of movement toward some new set or sets of relationships and in the uncertainties that a loosening of previous guarantees and understandings produces. A decay of the American alliance system in the Asian and the Pacific region, for instance, would not in and of itself breed its substitute as an ordering mechanism. In fact, since 1945 such an American system came into being, composed of the special bilateral United States–Japanese security agreements, the Australian–United States–New Zealand pact, the special American guarantees in Korea, and the American offshore military presence in the Pacific. These combined to be the umbrella under which existed postwar political relations among the "fringe states" of East and Southeast and South Pacific nations. Were such a presence drastically reduced, there would be no automatic substitute for it, even though such reduction of United States commitments seemingly might direct American resources and attention to domestic "priorities." While an immediate product of such actions could be a lessening of tensions between mainland China and America, the readjustments of foreign policies of other states would set in motion prospects of conflicts endangering international peace in new ways. The same logic would apply were the American presence in Europe greatly reduced. The uncertainty that such *détentes* produce is

[2] "New Balance of Power in Asia," *Foreign Affairs*, July 1971, p. 678.

not an augury of greater stability; in uncertain conditions, the foreign policies of states themselves become hard to predict, and many things that seemed previously impossible under conditions of "tight bipolarity" might revive as possibilities.

Thus it is that in the stream of events, following the decay of a bipolar world configuration, no particular ordering of state relations springs into being to take its place. The great powers, instead, confront each other in looser configurations; trust, the product of an understood system of bipolarity and of agreed perception about the patterns of configurations of world politics, is replaced by an awareness of each nation's distinct search for its own security and for its own national interests. As George Canning, British foreign secretary, wrote after the Holy Alliance had disintegrated in the 1820s, "Things are getting back to a wholesome state again: every nation for itself, and God for us all."

CHOOSING REQUIRES FORECLOSING OTHER OPTIONS

In foreign policy, as in other areas, some choices are forced by the limits of resources, others are forced by limits of options. Statesmen, even if equipped with a wide range of policy instruments, still may find themselves in circumstances in which choices must be made among incompatible policy goals. In such circumstances, choosing one turning at a crossroads forecloses the other; the choice once made, if it is not irrevocable, sets in motion a series of consequences that make it impossible to backtrack to the point where the choice was made. This is true even if the driver at the crossroads has a fine car and plenty of gas.

For instance, during the Suez crisis of 1956 the Eisenhower administration found itself in the painful position of having to choose between temporary abandonment of its chief NATO allies (Britain and France, which launched an attack upon Egypt to reopen the Suez Canal) or abandonment of its principles. The Anglo-French attack, however justified, clearly violated the UN Charter. Had the United States condoned or abetted this act, the price of loss of esteem in the non-European world would have been very heavy. Yet the (irrevocable) American decision, to demand that its chief allies cease aggression and withdraw, entailed heavy costs, risking imperilment of the great European coalition that deterred Soviet encroachments in Europe and the Mediterranean. This choice had to be made despite the existence of ample American resources at the time; its harshness was no consequence of scarcity but was intrinsic to a difficult situation presenting stark options. Another dilemma of the American government currently may be seen in the instance of Greece. Here, United States aid to one NATO ally, an authoritarian regime that has quaint and primitive views of civil order, seems repugnant to democratic values; yet forceful opposition to it or even the withholding of aid, might very well imperil NATO strategic objectives in the Eastern Mediterranean, since this regime, to sustain itself, might realistically accommodate itself to the Soviet Union or collapse in chaos (or both). The pursuit of virtue on a small scale in some circumstances may imperil larger, crucial strategic requirements, just as the virtuous pursuit of justice on a massive scale often has bred many particular tragedies. Nor is this simply an American dilemma. Many domestic critics of United States aid to the Greek junta also were among those calling for reconciliation with Communist China, though the latter's bloody record of travesties on civil freedoms and human life would be unimaginable in Greece. George Orwell, in his famous book about the Spanish Civil War, *Homage to Catalonia,* scourged the Soviet Union for condoning the Loyalist government's ruthless suppression of the 1937 Catalonian anarchists' uprising; yet Soviet motives then, in a strategic sense, were impeccable: a weakening of the Loyalist regime then, entailing the likely prospect of a subsequent fascist victory, would have added another fascist regime on the borders of Republican France, its needed ally. Thus, injustice done in a local "leftist" quarrel had a larger "leftist" rationale.

Thus it is that regardless of amplitude of resources, policy choices in world politics in the best of times frequently are often made between two or more "goods"; in the worst of times, between two or more "bads." An effort to accommodate with one state or group of nations on perfectly good motives may forfeit friendship of others or block improvement of relations with them; reconciliation with adversaries can entail estrangement of friends. The well-intentioned statesman then, in dealing with adversaries and friends alike, must sharply distinguish between the motives of his own policies and the likely or possible perception of them by others. (Some Monday-morning quarterbacks after World War II, argued the *Realpolitik* case that the United States then should have pressed for a separate peace with wartime Germany, since the actual policy of unconditional surrender turned out to have, as consequence, the obliteration of Germany as a political entity in Central Europe and the creation of the power vacuum there, which, as seen in consequent events, became the occasion and place of the cold-war confrontation with Russia. Yet two could have played this game; one grave risk of such *Realpolitik* during the war was that of a separate Soviet peace with the Nazi regime.) A course of action premised on the wish to obtain some understanding with an adversary thus must be judged also in its effects upon friends and even upon the "adversaries of adversaries."

This acute difficulty introduces an element of great complexity into strategic choices. In a two-dimensioned cold war, where "gains" to one side have been usually perceived as "losses" to the other, this complexity has been obscured; in circumstances of *détente* between America and Russia and in circumstances of emerging "multipolarity," the difficulties are best seen in two special instances: America's Far Eastern policies and America's policies in and toward Western Europe. In both instances, the wish to ·obtain accommodation with an adversary, on either general or specific matters, naturally affects friendly states. This is not a matter unique to American statecraft but also applies to dilemmas of any sovereign state in a time of great fluidity of affairs.

AN AMERICAN IMPERIUM OF SUBSIDIES

Both during World War II and in the 20 years that followed it, no nation in world politics placed more physical resources behind its foreign policies than the United States or invested these as broadly in the international arena. These resources mostly went into national defense and into defense of allies, but they were also expended upon the construction of new political and economic systems of international order and upon vast systems of aid for economic recovery of older industrial states for the development of new ones. From the beginning, American resources were poured by way of the Marshall Plan into the infrastructure of a new West European economic order; the new structure of international economic order was established around the American dollar. Such was the favorable American balance, both of trade and payments, during this period, that the heavy outflow of American private capital investment, principally to other highly developed countries, at times seemed to forebode American technological dominion over the major trading nations of Europe and the Americas. The American know-how in advanced technology of computers, aeronautics, and nuclear energy, energized by high federal support, seemed to portend an indefinite lead for American basic scientific research. Many of these developments, being dependent on sustained congressional budgetary support, were sanctioned by a broad political consensus at home because of their strong implications of national defense; yet many such international programs, so funded, were nevertheless informed by gen-uine humanitarian motives in *Realpolitik* disguise. All in all, in foreign aid during this time, the United States contributed more than $143 billion to allied, friendly, and neutral nations. (Vast as this figure appears, even considering its spread over two decades, the grand total comes only to less than 15 percent of current annual American gross national product.)

Such ample funds gave to American diplomacy during these years a flexibility that sharply contrasted with that of all other nations; for even when the Soviet Union, after Stalin's death, modified its policies of international spoliation and entered the competition in foreign aid, it did so with a selective, tough frugality that confined its effects principally to a few non-Soviet bloc states—Egypt, India, and Castro's Cuba. If the United States became, during this time, an imperial nation—as some have seen it—the influence and control that this connoted was of a different character than most previous empires had enjoyed: an imperi-um of subsidies rather than of exploitation. This was especially true in the field of purely military aid, for the American input of strategic weapons and their logistical systems in Europe, for instance, permitted European nations the unusual luxury of basking under a United States umbrella, in a profitable condition of dependency.

This largesse was costly to the American taxpayer and led to a worsening balance-of-payments situation for America. But it did mean that Europe now possessed a reasonably integrated defense system dominated by no one European state (Germany, for instance), and thus did not have severe political connotations.

The chief rationales of these enterprises were a compound of prudent fear and of hopes. One such fear was not that of war but that of Europe dominated by the Soviet Union or even controlled by it; another, the prospect of Asia dominated by one or more totalitarian powers. Such fears—at the height of the cold war—yearly were fueled by specific crises; they were of the same order as those fears that had previously existed when the objects of American concern had been Nazi Germany and Japan. In those previous circumstances, the undesired strategic danger had not been much different—Europe and Asia, dominated by two quite militant superpowers, each contemptuous of and hostile toward the liberal values of American democracy. (Historical fate sometimes swings on a pendulous cord; so it was that, in 1941 and 1942, when the prospect of an Axis-controlled world was very great, the contempt and hatred visited on the liberal democracies by the fascists, if ideologically different, still was as intense as that later heaped upon them by Communist revolutionaries.)

A danger successfully deterred, a threat confined, in history often later looks like a bogeyman or a straw contrivance; thus a success in foreign policy may soon lead to a forgetting of the authentic strategic objects that the enterprise had successfully attained. In this respect, during the 1950s and 1960s, until the time of the Vietnam War, it might be said that American foreign policy seemed to obtain its principal ends. In Europe, Soviet-sponsored communism failed further to expand, being, in George Kennan's words, "contained." The object of American policy within Western Europe, to which these vast resources were expended, had been to restore European strength, in John F. Kennedy's words, to "make the world safe for diversity." So also in Asia, aside from Vietnam, by the end of the 1960s, the strategic difficulty seemed contained.

Yet what may be preserved or gained in the heat and passion of insecurity may be lost in slippage in times of seeming calm. The classic American negative attitude toward external commitments could reassert itself. A mission accomplished, force could be reduced or withdrawn. Yet what no one could tell, for sure, was the extent to which the strategic objects of American policy had been obtained. A defect of democracies, de Tocqueville once remarked, was their inability to pursue long-range designs and their easy deflection of random concern to other wishes. Since no one authoritatively could know to what degree these American inputs by now had established a self-sustaining, stable order of diversity, strategists might prudently decide that such inputs into the strategic balance would have to continue even though the supportive passions once inspired by fear had waned. Yet to others, the implications of such protracted and seemingly unending prudence became increasingly unpleasant. An indefinite and costly American hegemonial role in world politics was a bleak prospect. "Hegemony" is just another word for imperialism; defense-inspired imperialism has similar nasty connotations, as an expansionist and initiative imperialism, if what one rejects is the sustained national employment of superior influence.

This was so also because the stated hopes of American leaders, in sustaining American security policies, had offered a picture of radiant messianism that transcended mundane objects. A democratic society in great strategic duress may from fear expend much energy and attention on its own survival and may find superfluous any grander spiritual objects than these; yet strategic objects long pursued even in relatively quiet times are—if not boring—of such an abstract character as to inspire little popular fervor.

Typically, then, declaratory policies enlarge upon mundane strategic purposes; in the cold war, American declaratory policies partook of a messianist nature not unusual in American history. "Let every nation know," said President Kennedy in 1961, at the time of his inauguration, "whether it wish us well or ill, that we shall pay any price, bear any burden, meet any hardship, support any friend, oppose any foe, in order to assure the survival and success of liberty." This undifferentiated and "priceless" promise made by a new American President, was rhetorical-ly sharper than, though not qualitatively different from, universalistic pledges made by previous administrations (in the Truman Doctrine, in 1947, the United States pledged itself to help resist aggression by armed minorities and totalitarian states *wherever* it occurred). These universal-ist pledges were directed, not simply to the defense of free peoples, but also to more positive humanitarian goals. Again to quote Kennedy: "To those people in the huts and villages of half the globe struggling to break the bonds of mass misery, we pledge our best efforts to help them help themselves, for whatever period is required—not because the Commu-nists are doing it, not because we seek their votes, but because it is right." In the rhetoric of Lyndon Johnson, himself an American populist, it was intolerable that a rich America find itself some day like the rich white house on a hill, surrounded by a sea of misery; an object of American policy was to deflect this possibility by concerted economic and political measures.

So, in practice, American strategic and humanitarian goals focused, during times of sharp confrontation, upon the outside world. For 25 years, from 1940 through 1965, opinion polls indicated that significant majorities of polled citizens persistently thought foreign problems to have higher priority and salience than domestic ones. Beginning in 1965, the ratio was reversed; since then, the salience of domestic questions—of race, domestic poverty, integration, "law and order," urban crises—began again to take precedence over issues of world politics. The skills and motivations of a younger generation turned inward from the outside world, criticizing all of the assumptions on which American policy had been previously grounded. The power expended for strategic purposes by administrations since 1939 became seen, not as a means by which strategic ends could be attained, but as an intolerable end in itself; the governmental mechanisms developed and established to gain these political ends became viewed themselves as sources of evils. The messianistic thrust that in the previous two decades had spilled out onto the world as handmaiden of strategic security suddenly turned inward upon America itself: an introversion of imperialism that, frustrated in foreign objects, saw objects closer to hand as of more immediate and central importance.

SHAPING POLICY INSTRUMENTS TO TARGETS

In economic policy, a well-known theoretical proposition states that the number of policy instruments must be at least as great as the number of targets or objectives. If this is not so, it will not be possible to pursue all objectives simultaneously. Policy makers instead must choose among them: discarding some, modifying or postponing others, and establishing priorities among those that remain. In circumstances of scarcity, these can be very harsh choices.

The reduction of American resources in foreign policy—curtailment of foreign aid, troop withdrawals from Europe, strategic cutbacks in Asia, curtailment of technological research in defense, abandonment of the dollar as the international monetary standard, a lessened role in UN peacekeeping operations—may be seen either as a quantitative reduction in response to objective changes in international circumstances and needs or as a considered reduction of will. A gradual disengagement of resources and a return to a more single-minded pursuit of particular interests might be welcomed by those who came to see American aid as dollar imperialism or capitalist militarism; yet these might cause concern among others, who remained convinced that, even in circumstances of currently lessened tensions, the objective conditions in world politics objectively remained both dangerous and complex. For one thing, the reduction of resources would take the form of reducing the number of available policy instruments; or it might take the form of the qualitative deterioration of such instruments as to blunt them. In either event, the result would be reduction of options in circumstances hypothetical to the choice between passivity or spastic response. Even more important was the problem of the nature of will that lay behind any mix of instrumentalities; a national climate of indecision that locked policy makers in tight frameworks of political constraint might betray American credibility in a wide span of circumstances. As the *Guardian,* a British journal frequently critical of American policies, remarked in midsummer of 1971, "For those . . . who see a world in which the United Nations is still too weak and divided to replace military alliances, and in which too few other nations are prepared to take on part of America's burden . . . the drift towards disengagement will produce a slight feeling of chill."

To this question of American moods about world politics Chapter 7 addresses itself.

REVIEW QUESTIONS

1. Does the United States need an "ideology of its own" to undergird its ongoing international politics?

2. Is it possible to determine whether a multipolar world of independent states and regions would be safer and more stable than a bipolar one?

3. In his Farewell Address, George Washington urged his successors to avoid "permanent alliances" and to seek "friendship and commerce with all." Is such advice realistic in the late twentieth century?

4. In the wake of a bipolar world, what kinds of options might the United States have with respect to its alignment with other nations?

6 RACIAL PROBLEMS AND AMERICAN FOREIGN POLICY

Racial problems rank high among the current discontents in American society. Since the early 1960s, they have opened a wide range of questions all of which pertain to the relationship of particular minorities—American blacks, Mexican-Americans and Asian-Americans—to the broader American culture and its institutions. While, for the most part, these questions seem chiefly focused on domestic political questions, they raise critical issues with respect to foreign policy as well. This chapter, then, addresses itself to a principal question: In what way may racial tensions at home affect United States goals and power applications abroad?

As will be seen in later parts of this chapter, this is by no means a new question in American history. Almost since the founding of the American

This chapter has been adapted from Chapter 3 of *Racial Influences on American Foreign Policy,* edited by George W. Shepherd, Jr. © 1970 by Basic Books, Inc., Publishers, New York.

Republic, race and nationality conflicts have played a prominent part in American politics. The United States, at least since the late nineteenth century, has been a "nation of nationalities." All known ethnic groups in North America, even American Indians, at some point in time have been immigrants. Today, the United States—in terms of specific racial groupings—contains more blacks than any African country aside from Nigeria, more Jews than any other nation in the world, more Irish than Southern Ireland. Large communities of Poles, Italians, and Czechs retain strong communal identity. White Americans of North European extraction historically have dominated United States culture. In numbers, they constitute the preponderant population. Not surprisingly, their dominance was reflected in American politics and has also reflected certain perceptions of American cultural ties. The high degree of concern historically exhibited by the United States government toward major events in Europe reminds us of the fact that North America still is a continent chiefly colonized by Europeans.

Race relations in America often have reflected race and nationality conflicts abroad. At certain points in time, in fact, such conflicts have ignited powerful corresponding conflicts at home, complicating the search for a national consensus about a real national interest. In this respect, the United States is by no means unique. What is unique, however, is the enormous ethnic and cultural heterogeneity in America, exceeding in magnitude and complexity that of any other major nation except, perhaps, the Soviet Union.

In the current political climate of the 1960s and 1970s, in many nations strong popular demands surge forward for liberation, emancipation, and equal rights. In some instances, such demands take the form of collective claims for group self-determination, for independence, for secession, relative to some dominant culture. In other instances, claims are made for greater access to the dominant culture's privileges. The United States, if only because of its high degree of civic freedom, its conspicuous position in the world, and its traditional egalitarian ethos, has become again an example to the world of the delicate relationship between liberty and equality, order and justice. While claims to equality are now made on behalf of many types of groups, the strongest of such claims is now racial.

Most Americans have short memories about their nation's foreign policy. The mass media foreshorten this perspective by focusing heavily on immediate and spectacular current questions, but the habit was not invented by television. It is part of our national character to be present and future oriented. This habit has both positive and negative sides. Americans are not long on grudges. We may not be very forgiving, but we can be more immediately forgetful. We have trouble in sizing up new situations, often failing to perceive the background against which to place some new occurrence. What is new really seems new. This surely has been the case with what seems to be the recent escalation of race conflicts in the United States to the level of national politics, affecting both our foreign policy and our international relations.

However, in fact, multiethnic America frequently has faced foreign policy crises in which domestic race and nationality issues have loomed large. In the Mexican War of 1846 to 1848, large numbers of Irish Catholics actually defected to the other side, choosing as Catholics to defend what they regarded as a Catholic nation. Before World War II, as the political analyst Samuel Lubell has suggested, the social sources of American isolationism and antiwar sentiment were largely ethnic. Times of war or threatened war have classically been occasions when issues of race and nationality have most dramatically surfaced to public attention. Sharp cleavages of opinion and attitude have temporarily sundered the American public. Now that we experience a civil-rights "revolution," while engaging the remainder of our attention with a war, we must try to place this problem in a historical perspective.

Race and cultural quarrels are not newcomers to American foreign policy; but, until very recently, studies of their effect have been limited only to European, white as opposed to nonwhite, minority influence. Negroes, while playing a major role in American domestic history, were considered to have shed their African ties soon after they stepped from the slave ships; Orientals, Puerto Ricans, and Mexican-Americans also have played insignificant roles with respect to American foreign policy. The United States was an Atlantic nation. That she practiced economic imperialism in Latin America and acquired an empire in the Pacific was forgotten in the single-minded concentration on European affairs.

Let me explore briefly the ways in which European minority groups in the United States have influenced its foreign policy, for even this hypothesis has not always been accepted. Again, until recently, most students of race and ethnic relations in America assumed that domestic racial quarrels stopped at the water's edge. This ethnocentric view considered American race relations primarily in terms of problems that were uniquely American. Comparative sociologists and political scientists are rapidly revising this outlook and have offered theoretical perspectives with which to study the influence of race on foreign policies of all plural societies.

IRISH-AMERICAN ANGLOPHOBIA

One of the earliest as well as the largest non-WASP (white Anglo-Saxon Protestant) European ethnic groups to arrive in the United States was, of course, the Irish Catholics. In the seven years between 1847 and 1854, 1.2 million Irish were driven from their island home largely by severe economic hardships including the disastrous potato famine of 1848. By the end of the American Civil War, Irish people formed 7 percent of the total white population.[1] The percentage decreased somewhat after the waves of Eastern European immigrants during the 1880s.

Irish Catholicism, which has tended to be anti-British, "liberationist," and often chauvinist, has provided a perspective often at odds with dominant American views on foreign policy. Occasionally, it converged with such views. Some writers, like the late Louis Adamic, have suggested that the American Revolution relied heavily on this source of radical ethnic zeal, especially in northern seaboard cities. Quoting an English writer, Adamic noted:

> Of the Irish colonists in America, a large proportion everywhere stood foremost on the side of the Patriots. It seemed as if Providence had mysteriously used the victims of British cruelty to Ireland, the men whom her persecution had banished from the bosom of their own land, as the means of her final punishment and humiliation on a foreign soil.[2]

A one-track guideline, Irish opinion historically was consistently hostile to United States policies congenial to England and vice versa. It was often deaf to more general policy considerations, such as the national security of the United States through alliances. This was so, because for nearly 150 years, Irish independence was entirely an anti-British issue. The now-familiar hostility to "imperialism" in American society had its nineteenth-century origins less in Marxism than in County Cork and

[1] Peter Rose, *They and We,* Random House, Inc., New York, 1964, p. 30.
[2] Louis Adamic, *A Nation of Nations,* Harper & Row, Publishers, New York, 1944 p. 324.

Dublin, where its most conspicuous West European victims then resided.

Irish opinion exerted itself most strongly during and after World War I. Predictably, it opposed entry into war on the side of the British. Although Irish Catholics could not prevent American participation in the war, American Anglophiles went so far overboard in their support of the British war effort that Irish nationalists, led by Tammany Judge Daniel F. Cohalan, were able to effectively oppose United States ratification of the Versailles Peace Treaty and the Covenant of the League of Nations. Irish-Americans were particularly opposed to Article X of the Covenant, which guaranteed the territorial integrity of all member states. To them this insured the continued subjugation of Ireland. During 1919 and 1920, numerous organizations dedicated to Irish independence sprang up in the United States, including the American Association for the Recognition of the Irish Republic, the Irish Self-Determination Club, and the Friends of Irish Freedom.

The isolationist spirit of Irish-America coincided with the rise of the Sinn Fein movement in Ireland, which was largely financed from the United States. The American Commission on Irish Independence appeared at the Versailles peace talks to promote the Irish cause. Eamon de Valera, the newly named President of the Irish Republic, escaped mysteriously from his English prison and toured the United States shortly after World War I to arouse the American people against the treaty, later against the League, and in favor of Irish independence. He was extremely successful.

Again, anti-British isolationism was the single motivating factor behind Irish Catholic opinion before World War II, and it remained a strong force until it was submerged by the patriotic support for war after Pearl Harbor.

GERMAN-AMERICAN ISOLATIONISTS

German-Americans, who constitute the second largest European ethnic group in the United States, have had an effect on American foreign policy similar to that of the Irish. German immigrants came in three waves: before the Civil War, between 1865 and 1885, and in the twentieth century after World War I until the early 1950s. The creation of a unified Germany under Bismarck in 1870 spurred public celebrations in many American cities; but, unlike the Irish-Americans, German immigrants played no significant part in unification of their homeland. The mid-1880s clash of interests between Germany, the United States, and Britain over the administration of Samoa was the only substantial intervention on the part of German-Americans in American foreign policy during the nineteenth century. According to Louis L. Gerson,[3] their dissatisfaction with the tripartite Samoan settlement contributed significantly to the defeat of Grover Cleveland in the election of 1888.

The Anglophobic coalition with the Irish-Americans began in earnest in 1914 and continued substantially unabated at least until 1941. German-Americans were strongly isolationist and neutralist before both world wars. In a study of Woodrow Wilson, Arthur S. Link quotes the President as saying, "We definitely have to be neutral, since otherwise our mixed populations would wage war against each other."[4] In 1941, a United States government report showed that German ethnic communities voted in national elections during both wars for the interests of their fatherland, and that 90 percent of the German press in the United States was pro-Nazi. American entry into World War II again muted the divisive tendencies of the German-Americans. But as Lawrence H. Fuchs, in his study of minority groups and American foreign policy, summed up the effects of these two ethnic groups:

> The persistence of chronic German- and Irish-American Anglophobia during the past eighty years has been an important internal factor in the making of American foreign policy. Its total effect has been to stall presidents and secretaries of state in their efforts to implement what they perceived to be a harmony of English and American interests.[5]

THE "ETHNICS" AND UNITED STATES POLICY TOWARD RUSSIA

While Italian-Americans reacted similarly to German-Americans before World War II, immigrants from Eastern Europe—Poland, Russia, Rumania, and Czechoslovakia—have generally been strongly interventionist and pro-British. Eastern Europeans were relatively recent arrivals in

[3] Louis L. Gerson, *The Hyphenate in Recent American Politics,* University of Kansas Press, Lawrence, 1964, p. 51.
[4] *Ibid.*
[5] Lawrence H. Fuchs, "Minority Groups and Foreign Policy," in *American Ethnic Politics,* Harper & Row, Publishers, New York, 1968, p. 150.

America, coming in large numbers during the 1880s and reaching their peak of immigration in 1921. Before and during World War I, many groups sought to bring United States power to bear against imperial Germany, Austria, and Russia to liberate their home countries. Similar efforts were made during World War II and in the cold war, when Stalinist Russia had overrun Eastern Europe. The "captive nations" constituencies of recently arrived East Europeans came to represent, during the height of the cold war, the hard core of United States liberationism, which opposed the containment policy of the Truman administration and supported "rollback" efforts to force a showdown with Stalin and establish free governments in Eastern Europe.

The Jewish population in the United States represents a distinct ethnic group. The first immigrants, a handful of Sephardic refugees from Spanish-Portuguese persecution in Brazil, arrived in 1654. However, until the nineteenth century, Jews numbered only a tiny fraction of the total population. They began arriving in great numbers—from Germany and Austria, particularly—in the post-Waterloo period until after the failures of the liberal 1848 revolution. By far the largest group of Jewish immigrants came from Eastern Europe—Russia, Rumania, and Poland—between 1880 and World War I. In those 35 years, the American Jewish population, mostly of rural peasant stock, rose to 2.5 million. Finally, Nazi atrocities in German-held territory precipitated the most recent influx, estimated at about 10,000 annually from the early 1930s until shortly after World War II. This latest group was generally middle class and more highly educated than the earlier arrivals.

As might be guessed, the pattern of Jewish immigration has influenced the role of Jews in American foreign-policy matters. Before the nineteenth century, the Jewish population was too insignificant to have any appreciable effect on foreign policy. In fact, until the early years of the twentieth century, Jewish interest centered on only two areas of concern: (1) the repeal of discriminatory commercial treaties and (2) treatment of Jews in foreign countries. In both areas, Jews were only sporadically successful in making their views felt. In 1840, President Van Buren was persuaded to intervene diplomatically in Damascus to protect Jews accused of ritual murder. But in the 1857 "Mortara incident," despite mass meetings held in New York and other American cities, President Buchanan refused to intercede with the Pope on behalf of an Italian boy kidnapped by papal authorities from his Jewish parents.

Similarly, Jews were unable to force a change in a commercial treaty with Switzerland in 1855, which allowed the Swiss to expel American Jews without due process or proper protection for their financial interests. In the 1908 presidential election, the failure of Russia to honor American passports held by Jewish citizens became a campaign issue, but William Howard Taft failed to keep his promise to remedy the situation after his election.

Because of the enormous flood of foreign-born immigrants, Congress, beginning in 1897, tried to impose immigration restrictions, which would require literacy tests and certificates of character from the countries of origin. These bills, which would have effectively eliminated Jewish immigration, were vigorously opposed by American Jews and were successively vetoed by Cleveland, Taft, and Wilson. When Coolidge finally signed into law the Immigration Act of 1924, the scope of the restrictions had been substantially broadened to include most of the non-Northern European minority groups.

The success of Jewish-Americans in influencing foreign policy in the era since World War I has been more fully documented. Their aims have been twofold: to gather United States support for the establishment of the independent state of Israel and, since World War II, to gain admission to the United States for displaced Jews. The groups most concerned with the creation of Israel were the Zionist Organization of America, which numbered 250,000; Hadassah, the women's auxiliary; and the American Zionist Emergency Council, which was responsible for the overall coordination of various Zionist groups. The major anti-Zionist organization in the United States has been the American Council for Judaism.

Like most minority groups, Jewish-Americans have exerted their influence primarily through the electoral process. During the 1948 presidential campaign, the Jewish community successfully pressured both political parties to adopt Zionist planks in their party platforms. In a few local elections, with a large Jewish minority, candidates of both parties were forced to outbid each other in their enthusiasm for the new state of Israel, which frequently became the major issue in the campaign.

The overwhelming success in recent years of the "Jewish" position on the various Middle East questions has been attributed to the simple fact that there are few Arabs in the United States and quite a large number of Jews.

Throughout the twentieth century, Jewish-Americans have been considerably less isolationist, less military-interventionist, and more liberal in their foreign-policy outlook. Jews have more readily supported world government schemes, including the establishment of both the League of Nations and the United Nations; the Marshall Plan for Europe; and foreign aid. As might be expected, however, such support is not uniform within the Jewish population. A recent study of Southern Jews, by Alfred Hero, indicates that they are considerably less "Jewish" and more rigidly conservative on foreign-policy matters than their northern coreligionists.[6]

Several generalizations can be made about this historical experience of race and foreign policy in America before 1945.

Insofar as racial or nationality questions have arisen in the past to affect judgments on foreign-policy crises, they have done so within minority groups that without exception wished to be integrated into American society. The aspirations of European ethnic minorities have almost invariably been assimilationist. By way of contrast, ethnic minorities in many other parts of the world more typically have sought *protection from* the dominant culture, rather than *access to* its values.

In America before World War II, disputes among European ethnic groups about foreign policy invariably were triggered by foreign events over which nationality groups themselves had virtually no control. In this sense, these groups were passive victims of the nationality and nation-state conflicts that tore European society apart in the later nineteenth century, consummated in the racial horror of Hitler's time. Between 1939 and 1941, the locales of powerful isolationist pressures against Roosevelt's intervention policies were those states and regions with Irish and German populations. It should be pointed out, however, that by and large these groups were not pro-Nazi.

Since these European events were a chief source of America's domestic "tribal" tensions, their outcome in 1945 decisively affected subsequent American outlooks on foreign policy. The end of Hitler's Germany signified an enormous defeat for European racist and tribal doctrines. A new Western European ethos after 1945 was integrationist and antiracist. Also, the new threat of Soviet expansion through Central

---

[6] Alfred O. Hero, Jr., "Southern Jews, Race Relations, and Foreign Policy," *Jewish Social Studies,* vol. 27, pp. 213–235, October 1965.

Europe fostered an awareness among European nationality groups of a common threat they heretofore had not perceived. By the beginning of the cold war in 1947, nearly all the classic reasons for American interethnic fighting over foreign policy were gone.

The new controversies in American politics that arose after 1946 paradoxically reversed a previous ethnic situation. In the late 1930s, many continental hyphenates in the United States urged us to remain out of Europe's wars. In the late 1940s and early 1950s, the opposite was true—especially of those Central and Eastern European minorities: Poles, Czechs, Slovaks, Slovenes, and others, who now called for an active American policy in Europe—namely, for the liberation of their homelands, the "captive nations"—by means of a United States-sponsored "rollback." By 1952, groups such as these launched a strong attack against the Truman-Kennan policy of containment, a doctrine that implicitly rejected a push forward in favor of a holding strategy and thus tacitly recognized the fact of Soviet domination in Eastern Europe.

This phase of the American ethnic disputes over foreign policy ended, for all practical purposes, in the late 1950s. Probably, one could date its end at 1956—the time of the Budapest uprisings, when the terribly high price of United States military intervention (that is, a major war with the Soviet Union) was quite clear.

The classic cold war, however, has had a unique effect on the race factor in the foreign policies of all countries, but most particularly Russia and the United States. At its height, there was a close correspondence between military and political-cultural bipolarity in world politics. Russia and America then dominated the realm of strategic power politics; each also commanded its own combination of allies—nations, states, or movements. The principal point of confrontation lay in Europe and the Mediterranean area.

During this 15-year period of Soviet-American conflict between 1948 and 1963, certain basic principles of social organization were elevated to an unusually high point. The issues involved in their confrontation tended to be universal ones (democracy versus communism, capitalism versus socialism, freedom versus totalitarianism) or *Realpolitik* ones—that is, a simple power struggle between America and Russia.[7] Yet

---

[7] See Paul Seabury, *Rise and Decline of the Cold War,* Basic Books, Inc., Publishers, New York, 1967, chaps. 1–3.

whether the conflict was "universalist" or "realist," it tended greatly to subordinate themes of race and color. The pot, of course, called the kettle black: Americans have pointed to the fact that the Soviet Union itself has been an "imperialist oppressor" of nationalities within its borders and of nation states in its satellite areas. The Soviet Union has pointed up imperfections in American society, especially the problems of black Americans, as instances of "capitalist" oppression.

But what American liberalism and Soviet Maxism both shared, in part by virtue of their common intellectual origins, was a profound rejection of racist doctrines that had previously served to integrate, or disintegrate, European societies. As Marxism—classical or Stalinist—owed its principal philosophical origins in large measure to Enlightenment thought, so its integrative principles were based upon conceptions of social equality not fundamentally different from liberal ones in one crucial respect: their common stress upon human solidarity based upon commonly shared human, not racial, qualities. In this respect, both of them were "true" enemies of racist National Socialism in Europe. (One should not flatter Stalinist Russia too much: after all, the mortal victims of Stalinism, "traitors" and "class enemies," vastly outnumbered Hitler's "racist" victims. A Benthamite might wonder whether it is more pleasurable to perish in consequence of genocide or "classicide.") Both American liberalism and Soviet Marxism stressed ideas of a future shape of political things in which race and nationality at best would comprise building blocks for more comprehensive multinational groupings of states and movements. (Whatever the differences between political-cultural developments in Eastern and Western Europe after 1947, it certainly is true that Stalinist hegemony over the Eastern nations—Czechoslovakia, Bulgaria, Rumania, and Poland—brought some respite from the furious nationality struggles of the earlier period.)

Nevertheless, the bipolarity of the cold war carried within itself the seeds of its own destruction. Although the confrontation between Soviet Marxism and American liberalism during this period tended to subordinate most other conflict situations in the world, Soviet-American competition in the non-European world on balance tended to hasten greatly the process of European decolonization and successful independence of nonwhite peoples in Asia, Africa, and elsewhere.

The end of the classic cold war can be seen chiefly in the replacement of a condition of relative political bipolarity with one of political multipolarity. America and Russia are still the superpowers in a strategic sense: that is, in their capabilities for waging massive war. But in other respects, especially in their capacity successfully to manage great coalitions, they now have far less influence.

The new world of the post-cold-war era is a peculiar one in that some of its more visible characteristics might be said to be retrogressive, in terms of the classical expectations of Western liberalism and of Marxism. Retrogressive *and* "disintegrationist," one might add. Since the mid-1960s, irrespective of region, the world has been experiencing the revival of ethnic, tribal, and racial tendencies toward *apartheid.* This can be seen, in Europe, in renewed animosities between Northern Irish Protestants and Catholics, Flemings and Walloons, Welsh and English, Basques and Spaniards, Serbs and Croats, Czechs and Slovaks. In North America, it can be seen in mounting tensions between Quebeçois separatists and English-speaking Canadians, and in the color crisis in cities in the United States. In Asia, it can be seen in Communist China's sponsorship of "Third World" movements and ideologies and in its chauvinist expulsion of non-Chinese influences from its own territories. In Southeast Asia and the Indian subcontinent, the same tendencies are to be seen in clashes between Pakistanis and Bengalis, Chinese minorities and dominant majorities of Malays, and in the current crisis of the Indian government to maintain national unity among polyglot subcultures. The Middle Eastern crisis between Arab and Jew continues. In Africa, the immense massacres of blacks by Arabs in the Sudan, the Nigerian civil war, and the racial crisis in South Africa bear a bleak witness to the recrudescence of tribalism.

It is not reassuring to note that, in the non-Western and non-Communist world, attempts by some political leaders to create forms of solidarity among polyglot populations have involved the invocation of neocolonial specters, anti-Western and in some instances antiwhite ideologies. It certainly is clear that no particular nation—developed or underdeveloped—has a monopoly on these discontents. Western Europe perhaps has been the most immune from them, although the racial tensions in England between new Commonwealth immigrants and "nativists" suggest otherwise.

This international revival of ethnic-racial discontent is conditioned by crosscurrents not explicitly racist. Many followers of Franz Fanon have concluded that there should be an immense "revolt against the West" by long-suppressed proletarian cultures—that is, an inevitable rebellion against "whites" by "all those others." Suspicious Russians may perceive the old spook of the "yellow peril" more vividly than others. Many guilt-laden intellectuals, both in America and elsewhere, now portray the emerging "crisis" as one between a heartless technological civilization of Northern Hemispheric nations and the nontechnocratic, backward nations to the south. A good deal of *mea culpa*, floating around Europe and America both, seeks to blame Western nations for the sorry plight of poverty-stricken, famished, and overpopulated backward nations. But the revival of racism simply cannot be seen as a mere function of economic inequality, "West" versus "Third World," technology versus humanism, or "rich North versus poor South." Another point must be made: these tribal, racial conflicts are modified or held in check in important ways by countervailing influences, including realistic assessments of the prices to be paid and the horrors to be experienced from pursuit of tribalist policies. One recoils from the specters of massacres, forced population transfers, and South African pass systems. And yet one somehow continues to believe in the possibilities of human coexistence in freedom under nondiscriminationist systems of constitutional law.

How do such new developments affect the problem of America's relationship to its outside environment? How important today are race, ethnicity, and hyphenate nationality in public attitudes toward America's foreign policies?

The first thing to note is that America is less and less a multiracial society; ethnic tensions among whites today play probably a smaller role than ever before in day-to-day American politics. America no longer is a nation of immigrants. Even the "Catholic issue" has virtually disappeared as a political issue. Some intellectuals may deny it, but it is still true that a Southern white populist from Texas—Lyndon Johnson—managed to command strong political support even in the North and even among Northern Negroes. There is now no particular reason why a Jew or a black cannot run on a presidential ticket. The iron law which said that an Irish Catholic could not be elected President turned out to be rather mushy when put to the test in 1960. The foreign-policy establishment in Washington, which once was regarded as a special preserve of eastern, white, Protestant, rich, college-educated Anglo-Saxons from Yale, Harvard, and Princeton, has now given way to a complex ethnic mélange more distinguished by its expertise than simply by its growing diversity. Charles de Gaulle continued to regard America as an Anglo-Saxon country, conspiring with England to subjugate the Gauls and other more cultivated peoples. But American WASPs would wonder.

RACE AND FOREIGN POLICY

So we are now left with the question of the American blacks and American foreign policy. I say it this way, rather than, for instance, the American blacks and the Indochina conflict. It would be a mistake to become hypnotized by one occasion of conflict, to the exclusion of all other facets of America's international interests, commitments, and purposes. Also, there is no such thing as an endless war. Some day, this one will end. But the problems of American blacks in American society will go on for a very long time; and these problems will inevitably occur in a larger world context in which nonwhite races share with American blacks the problem of poverty in a world of potential abundance and technical productivity. Other issues, crises, and problems will follow Vietnam and command our attention. Civil rights, economic opportunity, and racial discrimination will be with us for quite some time.

It is, however, because the civil-rights revolution and the Vietnam War accidentally coincide that we should examine their relationship and the symbolic ramifications of both of them at this point in time.

Beginning in the late 1960s, some observers have sought to read into the Vietnam conflict certain cultural and ethnic connotations, whose logic would exist even were there no civil-rights problem in America at all. There have been two principal schools of thought about this, existing in uneasy and inexplicit alliance with each other, and both highly critical of American involvement in this war. Yet the underlying judgments and evaluations of each are markedly different.

A first school of thought, perhaps most explicity circulated by Walter Lippmann, has sought to convey the impression that what happens in Asia, to Asian peoples, is insignificant; that America is an "Atlantic" nation, and its real ties are with the more advanced countries of Europe. John K. Galbraith, our former Ambassador to India, made a similar point, too, when he remarked in 1966 that Vietnam was, after all, an "insignificant" little country and hardly worth paying attention to. Real culture, and real affinities, lie elsewhere.

Inversely, others have argued that "white" Americans, or white men generally, have no longer a "right" to be in Asia or, for that matter, in any other nonwhite area of the world. The future of Asia belongs to Asians. The day of the "white man" in these parts of the world is over and gone, just as Rudyard Kipling is gone. This doctrine, a kind of reverse *apartheid* argument, is frequently shouted by some in the American New Left. Its domestic implications for a so-called white society, where nonwhites—including many Asian-Americans—are a minority, are not mentioned.

Yet whatever else it may be, the conflict in Vietnam has not been an ethnic war. Both sides are composed of complex coalitions of nations and of ideological movements. On our side, in addition to the multicultural forces of Vietnam opposed to Hanoi's brand of communism, are the United States, New Zealand, Australia, Thailand, the royalists and neutralists of Laos, the Philippines, and South Korea. Material support comes from many other countries of Asia and Europe. On the "other side," are the Vietcong and the North Vietnamese government, which is aided by China, the Soviet Union, "white" East European communist regimes, and many other communist movements. It should be clear that Vietnam cannot simply be seen either as a racial war or as an "Asian" war. It has been a civil war within an Asian country, with widely recognized international implications for the delicate balance between the Communist world and ours. The civil-war aspect long since has been overridden by the international one, and this is *not* an ethnic one.

While the basis of the Vietnam conflict is not racial, it is not entirely accidental that the war should coincide with heightened race problems in the United States. These are immensely complex events, with more than one point of conjuncture and interaction. Looking at the economic effects of the war on the so-called war on poverty, one immediately notes at least two contradictory effects. Vietnam has occasioned, and certainly served as excuse for, substantial cuts in federal antipoverty programs. But since American wars characteristically have hastened the pace of racial integration, Vietnam is not necessarily an exception to this rule. It *is* true that proportionately more American blacks than whites have served in combat situations in the war. But—regardless of the complex moral issue of inequity that this poses—this in itself as in the past will probably hasten, rather than retard, the process of ethnic integration by serving as a surrogate college education for the economically deprived, as all recent major American military engagements have done.[8]

Looking at the political interrelationships between Vietnam and the civil-rights movement, one can also see contradictory patterns. It is true that the war has been an occasion for extremist racist groups to exploit dissatisfactions. It has given Black Power devotees and even more fanatical sects a chance to link demagogically their separatist causes to a larger issue. No doubt some racist ideologues see the Negro ghetto as only one of many battlegrounds of struggle against "Washington imperialism." Some moderate civil-rights leaders have drawn quite different implications from both theaters; convinced as they have been of the moral authority of nonviolent action, they have logically—if unrealistically—sought to apply their own norms of social action to the Vietnam conflict. Finally, the style of disobedience, applied with such success to resist illegal and unconstitutional white racist authorities in the South and elsewhere, has spilled over into the larger theater of national politics and foreign policy as a multipurpose if dangerous device for redressing any grievance, real or fancied, and any law, constitutional or otherwise.[9] The style and tactic no longer are confined to legitimate ethnic issues and grievances or, for that matter, to specifically ethnic issues.

Yet at the same time, we note contradictory evidence: as opinion polls pointed up after 1965, the popularity of the Johnson administration among American blacks as a whole was not significantly different than among other Americans. At times, during the Vietnam War, it was in fact even higher. More blacks than whites, furthermore, support the Vietnamese War (though it should be pointed out that, among college-educated blacks, the rate of dissent appears slightly higher than among their white equivalents).

The reason for this may not be hard to find, nor surprising. The Vietnam War coincided with the greatest legislative breakthrough on civil rights and racial equality in American history. American blacks would certainly have been peculiar if they had responded toward the Johnson administration in any different fashion than they did. Much of the racial violence in American cities may be due to the disparity

[8] See Morris Janowitz, *The Professional Soldier: A Social and Political Portrait,* The Free Press, New York, 1960.
[9] But peace marches in American cities significantly have had very few blacks in them; neither have the "patriotic" parades.

between expectation and fulfillment and between administration prom ises and existing realities. But if we read the polls correctly, American blacks rate the domestic issue of equality of opportunity far higher than they rate the importance of Vietnam, one way or another. There probably is no higher proportion of idealists among blacks than in other parts of American society; but I would hazard the guess that there are substantial numbers of realists among them.

The marathon Arab-Israeli hostility among other things reminds us that the world of international politics contains many risks other than Vietnam. So, too, our own preoccupation with this particular conflict should make us aware that there most certainly will be more limited wars in our future. This is not the last generation that will run the risk of involvement in collective violence for some purpose or other. If this is a reasonable guess, we must now ask: How may America's "racial politics" gear into future features of our foreign policy?

An *apartheid* America, in a world of other racial strains and stresses, will be unable to participate effectively and constructively in an international community. An America that persists toward closer integration and equality of opportunity regardless of race, religion, or color, will remain what it has been until now, something of an example to others. On the other hand, an America sharply divided between blacks and others will be a disastrous example to other nations, just as once, a generation or so ago, American successes in "solving" its ethnic problems among its European nationalities served as a positive and constructive example to Europe.

Looking only at our past successes in foreign policy, they have, on the whole, been ones that came from acting in close constructive tasks with wide groupings of other nations. America's effectiveness in such enterprises has sprung not simply from the abundance of the resources we had to put in them nor from the credibility of the promises and commitments we made. It also has depended upon our "openness" and willingness to tolerate, even encourage, diversity—and on our credible reputation as a "nation of nations," which had richly incorporated in itself more foreign influences than perhaps any other major country has ever done. In a world that everywhere shows new signs of revived racial stresses and tensions, an American failure would have deep consequences not only for ourselves but also for the future of open societies in general. In retrospect, this crisis has far greater import than the

European ethnic crises that America once experienced in a world that once seemed to be exclusively run by whites, but that now is not.

REVIEW QUESTIONS

1. How may contemporary American race relations differ, in their effects on American foreign policy, from their influence in previous periods of United States history?

2. How may transnational ethnic ties affect domestic views of United States national interests? Can an American national interest be free from transnational sentiments and affinities?

3. In the 1950s, many "ethnic Americans" of Eastern European descent demanded that the United States assist in the "liberation" of their "homelands" from Soviet domination. Today, some American blacks demand United States support for black independence in South Africa. What validity do both of these claims on American power have?

4. Given the multiethnic character of the American population, what national strengths and advantages flow from it in our foreign relations?

7 ON ALLIANCES AND COMMITMENTS

Is the United States today "overextended" in the span and intensity of its involvement in world politics? This question, rarely raised in public during the harsh phase of bipolar conflict between the United States and the Soviet Union, became a matter of public dispute in the 1960s, when fears of major thermonuclear war between the superpowers subsided, and when the United States became actively engaged in a second protracted war on the Asian mainland. Then and now, the United States stands at the center of a complex network of alliances; some are bilateral, others multilateral. A principal justification of these has been that they serve American security interests; they serve to maintain conditions of peace and order in which American democracy can flourish. Yet the alliances have had their price. Twice in two decades, Americans have paid the price of major involvement in geographically localized war, in Korea and Southeast Asia. Continuously, since the mid-1950s, the United States has paid a great material price to sustain these commitments. Resources have been taken away from internal needs. Some have argued that this price was worthwhile: international stability and therefore peace have been strengthened by the known force that America was willing to place on the line to deter aggression in areas deemed crucial to its own interests and to those of its principal allies, the democratic and open societies of East Asia and Western Europe. Yet the argument for such large and extensive commitments is a novel one in American history: the conventional wisdom of American foreign policy before 1939 lay in abstaining from any overseas alliances and from any continuing political role in the affairs of the non-American world, aside from East Asia.

In practice, the United States in recent times has not been the "world's policeman." There are significant parts of the world where United States influence plays little part in normal ongoing political events and where American power has been withheld in times of conflict. Yet the rhetoric of American diplomacy, since the late 1940s and until the Nixon administration, tended to stress the universal role that American force and influence should play in maintaining international peace and in defending "free nations" against aggression. United States hegemonic military influence remains strong and self-evident both in the Pacific and in Western Europe. Its alliance ties with Japan and European NATO countries remain close.

Now, when world politics seems more fluid than at any time since the 1930s, it would be useful to ask what criteria Americans might employ in determining the span and intensity of United States influence in world politics. But also, to raise more compelling questions: When do nations prosper better with allies, when without them? What risks and benefits might a nation derive from aiding or abandoning allies? How does one go about determining the relationship between such foreign commitments and the resources necessary to underwrite them?

Often in our national history, Americans have quarreled over the proper extent of the external influence of the nation, the nature of American foreign commitments to other states, and the costs of involvements. In the twentieth century we may discern at least four occasions of major debate over these questions. It is by no means accidental that these occasions have been coincident with international wars: 1917 to 1919; 1939 to 1941; 1950 to 1952; and, since 1965, the occasion of the Vietnam War. In other times of greater tranquility, the general architecture of the political world is taken for granted; and it is paradoxical that, in as dynamic a nation as America, strong forces have periodically sought to restrain America's outward expansion. In times of trouble, however, when the universe of politics becomes uncertain and deranged, the quarrels over American purposes occur most dramatically; "necessity" may bring an end to debate, as was the case after the Japanese attack on Pearl Harbor in 1941. But in most instances during the twentieth century, we see that the circumstances inspiring the debate were chiefly not of America's own choosing. Rather they were products of a complex chain of circumstances in which American options and actions were not free but were dependent on the acts of others.

Before 1939, the chief fulcrum point of American debates over foreign affairs was its historic policy of abstention from alliances with other states. But now, and ever since the mid-1960s, the issue has revolved, instead, around the extent, character, and magnitude of United States commitments, rather than on the question of whether they should exist at all. The new debate, spurred by the inconclusive Vietnam War, has been no more bitter than previous ones, but it has split American society in new ways on the subject.

History offers no useful analogies to the American alliance system that came into being after World War II. On a smaller scale, more than 2,000 years ago, the Athenian Delian League of Greek city-states bore resemblance to it, and Thucydides the historian should be referred to for the particulars. But this was on an infinitely smaller geographic scale than the American system; in this, after World War II, there came to be an American-centered multiple system of alliances: the Rio de Janeiro Pact; the North Atlantic Treaty Organization; the Southeast Asia Treaty Organization; and more special alliance arrangements: the bilateral Japanese-American security pact; the Australian–New Zealand–United States treaty; and many bilateral arrangements with individual states. The span of these arrangements, which have ranged from Southeast Asia eastward to Berlin, from the South Pacific to the northernmost tip of Norway, suggest the complexity of these arrangements. The scope magnitude, and multiplicity of America's ties with allies have no real precedent in history. Great alliance systems have existed in the past, but this one—multiple, extensive, and hegemonic—must supply its own logic. Its own experience, alone, can offer instructive lessons for future conduct.

The idea of commitment has two distinct meanings: a promise or obligation entered into, as in an *alliance;* and the actual employment or intent to employ force in specific circumstances and situations. The two meanings, although closely related, are by no means the same; for in the latter sense we speak of an act, or of an intention to act, that may or may not arise from an obligation previously incurred. A nation may have declaratory and unilateral commitments that are not contractual: for example, the Monroe Doctrine. It may also incur contractual commitments to other nations, obliging it to act in certain ways in certain kinds of contingencies. In peacetime, the promissory character of the relationship is pointed toward important future hypothetical situations. The promissory commitment, even when prompted by motive of deterrence, paradoxically cannot be wholly credible until a *casus foederis* arises: the situation in which the promise is fulfilled, when deterrence, so to speak, "fails."

BALANCING RESOURCES AND COMMITMENTS

Walter Lippmann, in his book, *U.S. Foreign Policy: Shield of the Republic,*[1] framed the notion of an ideal set of norms by which the viability of a nation's foreign policy might be determined. Writing in 1943, he argued that a nation can be said to have a foreign policy only when a balance is struck between that nation's resources and its foreign commitments. When commitments were extended beyond available national resources, then a nation had no foreign policy. The task of statecraft was to bring commitments and resources into balance, while seeking to acquire a "comfortable surplus of power" to back up the nation's security obligations. It was Lippmann's argument that an imbalance of commitments and resources had existed, for America, ever since the Spanish-American War; for that war, resulting in a vast enlargement of our commit-

---

[1] Little, Brown and Company, Boston, 1943.

ments in the Pacific, entailed no commensurate increase in our power to back them up. The implications of this imbalance had not been grasped until it was too late to prevent war with Japan.

This commonsense formula could apply to both contractual and declaratory commitments. No one would ever wish to overextend his obligations beyond his ability to sustain them. Yet this idea of balance is too simple. The hardest task is not to achieve an equilibrium of commitments and resources, but to determine the appropriate level and magnitude of the equation. One might think a nation *overcommitted* or *undercommitted* even when there did exist a balance between means and aims. Whether one should seek equilibrium at a high or a low level cannot be determined merely by the equation itself. When commitments are "high," one increases the reserve of power to back them up. But, some would ask, why so high? If commitments are low, why so low? Obviously, the appropriateness of any particular level of commitments must depend upon judgment about the specific requirements of international and domestic politics. Necessity may dictate a certain level of commitments far beyond available resources—a bad situation, of course, yet one that might be unavoidable.

WASHINGTONIANS AND JEFFERSONIANS

Advance promissory arrangements with allies are not the necessary preliminary to wars and certainly not to American wars. Only once in its history has the United States become involved in war arising out of previous treaty commitments: Vietnam! The American tradition of abstention from alliances, broken in 1947 and 1949 by the Rio and NATO treaties, was no guarantee of peace. If anything, the doctrine of abstention, in the twentieth century, meant that the United States' entry into conflicts tended to be late and total rather than early and limited. One price for abstention from early stages of conflicts was that situations could deteriorate to a point where *major* conflict, world war, might occur. More timely intervention would permit greater control over the movement of events, yet, of course, increase the frequency of conflict involvement.

The American theory of isolationism practiced before World War II contained a basic ambiguity. Most Americans misunderstood the meaning of Washington's Farewell Address, confusing its message with that of Jefferson. The essential parts of the Farewell Address were actually drafted by Alexander Hamilton. It was *permanent* alliances that Washington warned against, while Jefferson deprecated *entangling* ones. The advice of Washington was a prescription for national flexibility and maneuverability, not for inaction and passivity.

His injunction against permanent commitments, friendships, and animosities was consistent with the classic eighteenth-century rules of European *Realpolitik*. The Jeffersonian warning, with its stress upon entanglements, spoke of undesirable substantive outcomes of contractual commitments, particularly the risk that mingling American purposes with those of other states would severely limit American freedom of action and would lend our resources to exploitation by other states.

Failure to distinguish between these two prescriptions has periodically caused confusion about our foreign policy. There were really two isolationist traditions. The Washingtonian version was espoused by conservatives and nationalists like Senators Henry Cabot Lodge and Arthur Vandenberg in the 1920s and 1930s. The Jeffersonian tradition in this century has belonged to liberals and progressives intent on minimizing foreign involvements in order to stress domestic priorities. Traditionally, Jeffersonian liberals have been fearful of the domestic costs of sustained, active involvement in world politics and suspicious of the expansion of executive branch power that occurs in foreign emergencies.

Today's American commitments depart from both Washingtonian and Jeffersonian principles. The credibility of the several alliance systems to which the United States is joined depends upon their assumed semipermanence as a set of priorities for action. It is doubtful if it could be otherwise: to assume that our contractual alliances were simply temporary conveniences would be to detract from their ongoing credibility. They would have little deterrent effect if it were thought that they could be readily broken or abandoned. Whether or not we should ever have undertaken these obligations or whether the undertaking of so many of them resulted in an overextension of American resources (thus violating the "Lippmann doctrine"), the inherent logic of the alliances currently lies in their *systemic* character. The easy flexibility of eighteenth-century alliances and alignments—reflecting the condition of European politics in Washington's time—is a far cry from the situation that obtained in world politics after the cold war had commenced.

To remind ourselves of the founding fathers' advice today is to be aware of the fact that neither the Jeffersonian nor the Washingtonian doctrine was proof against the possibility of action commitments. Until Vietnam, no war in which America became involved was entered for promissory reasons. No treaty obligations triggered American belligerency in World Wars I and II. In Korea not only was there no previous promise; there was even a previous assumption shared by the Joint Chiefs, the State Department, and General MacArthur that Korea lay *outside* the United States defense perimeter. Only the event itself—the 1950 North Korean attack—triggered the response. The absence of prior commitments was no guarantee against United States involvement, or indeed, against United States "overextension" in subsequent conflict. This is not to say that the existence of contractual agreements does not multiply the possibilities of potential large-scale future conflict. *It is simply that one cannot really know,* in the abstract, whether or not this is the case.

LESSONS OF THE 1930s

After 1945, two basic assumptions underlay the alliance network that America joined and helped to devise. One was the "arm's-length" doctrine; the other was what could be called the Manchurian assumption. The arm's-length doctrine meant that American security was best maintained by keeping potential enemies as far from the North American continent as possible. A purely military doctrine, it came to have two corollaries—first, that an Asian equilibrium could be sustained only by permanent United States participation in it; and second, that a European equilibrium must be established. In both theaters, no one power should be permitted to dominate, for this would threaten American security.

This was related to an interpretation of World War II, the Manchurian assumption. It was thought that the peril America faced from 1941 to 1945 was largely the result of our passive foreign policy in the 1930s, when the interwar system deteriorated. By not actively manipulating specific small international crises, America permitted them to accumulate into a grave threat. The long road from Japan's invasion of Manchuria led inexorably to the Rhineland, from the Rhineland to Ethiopia, from

Ethiopia to Munich, and from Munich to major war in 1939. Each unchecked aggression was additive. An active America might have employed its deterrent influence, and World War II might have been avoided. The Manchurian assumption thus became the implicit rationale for America's postwar alliances. The "domino theory" derives from it: If aggression undeterred is aggression enhanced, then the "fall" of one domino will mean the fall of another ad infinitum.

The arm's-length doctrine and the Manchurian assumption called for an *early* and *intimate* involvement in conflict situations on the assumption that only thus could they be contained. In theory, of course, this did not necessarily require the making of contractual commitments. A "free hand" can be an active hand without engaging in an embrace or handshake. But the lessons of the 1930s did seem to teach the need for a wide-ranging diplomacy and a willingness to threaten in order to deter.

PRIORITIES OF OBLIGATION

The uniqueness of the American commitment system constructed after World War II can be seen in the following combination of qualities: its hegemonial nature (for the immense power of the United States made it *primus inter pares*—first among equals); its plurality (being not one, but several distinct security systems, each playing itself out in a different region of the world among a different cast of characters); its ultimate reliance on American force (in each alliance, United States military power was the key); and finally its geopolitical rank ordering (for few doubted the primacy of the West European-Mediterranean commitment in the hierarchy of United States interests or the magnitude of resources made available to it). In each separate alliance, the United States contribution has been the main one, with the resources flowing outward from the North American continent. It was the power of the Soviet Union and the states and movements associated with it, as well as their tendency toward forcible expansion, that brought the American security system into being and supplied its essential logic. That the Communist world became polycentric, while the Soviet Union tended to become more conservative as it grew more powerful, did not essentially alter the expansionist goals of individual Communist governments. Forged to constrain this expansion, the American alliance system has been sustained in its purpose by defensiveness, reactiveness, and prudence.

But the unwieldy scope of United States commitments caused problems from the beginning. How were the disparate alliances to be interconnected? Though Washington has naturally wished to make its separate alliances compatible, each of them has embraced different countries with different interests in different parts of the world. Obligations in Europe were not binding in Asia, yet the American presence on both continents would necessarily establish a relationship between them. United States performance toward one set of allies would affect resource allocation elsewhere. This has worked both ways. The Korean War in 1950 set in motion an American-European mobilization that bolstered Europe's defenses, but the Vietnam War operated in opposite fashion, reducing United States contributions to NATO and probably encouraging Soviet gambles in the Middle East and Mediterranean. The risks incurred in fulfilling one set of commitments can weaken others, either by suggesting that some allies are being downgraded or that they may involuntarily be dragged into a conflict not of their choosing.

In each alliance, the degree of deterrent credibility has hinged upon the credibility of the United States. Under what circumstances would the honoring of one set of commitments enhance another? Under what circumstances would the dishonoring of one weaken the others? Are commitments taken as a whole divisible or indivisible? Are there ever occasions when honoring one commitment might undercut another?

These questions of credibility raise more practical questions of priority. Though the United States might set a rank order of priorities among its regional alliances ("Europe first," for example), that rank order could not with any certainty reflect the sequential order of commitment fulfillment. Since World War II, the American commitment to Western Europe has been fundamental; yet the only occasions when United States commitments have been "called" in a shooting war have been in Asia—Korea and Indochina. When the commitment system is challenged, the hegemonial power has to decide whether to honor (or dishonor) a particular commitment, even though it may not have "high" priority. Indeed, an inherent difficulty in the alliance system is the likelihood that challenges are more likely to occur, not in its "central theater," but on its peripheries, where the risk of general war is less great.

A third, and now most acute, problem concerns the central role of the hegemonial power. While many other states are joined with America in sustaining *one* particular defense system, America is joined in them all. Locked as it is into each system, the armed forces of the hegemonial power are bound to be committed to battle more frequently than the forces of its partners, on the assumption that conflicts remain localized. Since World War II, United States forces have fought in major wars twice, while the Soviet Union has avoided involvement, limiting its role to one of material and ideological aid to its allies.

REBALANCING ALLIANCES

If we indeed face a period of continued danger and insecurity, it is time to rethink the purposes of our postwar alliance system. In 1951, during the Senate debate over the President's authority to commit United States troops in Europe, the prevailing view of our legislators was that American aid was a temporary expedient designed to foster the self-defense of Europeans. Senator Henry Cabot Lodge proposed at the time that the dispatch of American troops be contingent upon a certification by the Joint Chiefs of Staff that our allies were doing their utmost to provide for their own defense and were supplying the bulk of NATO ground forces in Europe.

But the tensions of the period, including the Korean War and memories of the Berlin blockade, gave rise to a second and quite different conception of NATO. That alliance and others were seen in the ideal as interposing a massive counterforce to Russian and Chinese power. They were to be the locus for American advance bases, conceived as the major bolstering element in Western defense. This conception prevailed, and the United States assumed the role of *primus inter pares* in all its alliances. Our allies, seeing a high proportion of their defense costs borne willingly by the United States, were reluctant to tax their own economies by taking the main share of the burden for themselves.

Senator Lodge's approach of 1951 is being rediscovered in the 1970s. Self-help was the main theme of President Nixon's first foreign policy report to Congress. A new balance is being sought, for the post-Vietnam reevaluation of United States foreign policy, which began in 1969, has reopened the question of the entire American alliance system. Reconsidering commitments is the first step toward American movement from a *primus inter pares* role toward that of an "equal among equals," a *parus inter pares.*

President Nixon called for a more "mature partnership" with Western Europe, less United States dictation to Latin America, and a more responsible role for Asian nations in their own defense. Significantly, he described the Nixon Doctrine not only as a means for more effective sharing of common resources, but also as the "American policy which can best be sustained over the long run." There is recognition of the urgent need for retrenchment in our world security role, lest the nation slide into isolationism in reaction to Vietnam and there be reckless miscalculation on the part of our overseas opponents. The *Time*-Harris poll of 1969 revealed that 64 percent of the American people felt that if the United States is to defend weaker countries at all, it must do so in conjunction with our principal allies. By nearly 2 to 1 (52 percent to 28 percent), Americans agreed: "We cannot go it alone in the world any longer."

A more equitable partnership could diminish the strain on United States resources, allowing for more to flow toward pressing domestic needs and thereby lessening potential isolationist pressures. It is in this sense the policy that can best be sustained over the long run. Because it can be sustained, it will tend to add stability to the current highly unstable environment by more closely equating American obligations, not so much with what the nation is *able* physically to do, as with what it is *willing* to do in a period of domestic upheaval.

If the hegemonial power ceases to be hegemonial, that may, of course, decrease the credibility of its alliances. The game theorists tell us that if one succeeds in making one's opponent identify a particular object as directly relating to one's own national security, then the first step toward a credible commitment has been taken. The defense of Paris relates directly to the national interest of the French, Bangkok to that of the Thais, Tokyo to that of the Japanese. Since many Americans are unwilling today to support security guarantees to any of these allies, it would increase the credibility of the entire alliance system if our partners reaffirmed their own central concern with their own defense in this time of domestic American troubles.

This is not to say that the United States will cease to be generally hegemonial. The power realities of economics and nuclear weapons are such that the United States would vastly predominate in any alliance combination, except in the unlikely case of an alliance with the Soviet Union. But in specific regions of the world and in conventional arms this need not be the case. The conventional military potential of America's allies in any particular region far outweighs any force the United States can expend, given the diffusion of its power around the globe. The problem remains one of getting our allies to play conventional yeoman to America's nuclear knight.

Thorny command and control problems may make partnership difficult. By becoming a more "equal" ally, could not the United States be dragged into a war against its will and best interests? Theoretically this is possible, though the escape clauses in the nuclear nonproliferation treaty and the stipulation in our defense treaties that United States intervention occur only "in accordance with constitutional process" offer a way out.

These are good reasons why the United States should pull back to play a more modest role in its present alliance system. First, a higher interest compels modification of our hegemonial activism abroad, and that is the need to employ our resources at home. Second, as the alliances have grown incrementally over the past 23 years, the United States at no point ever really committed itself to the preponderant *conventional* military role that it now occupies.

Third, we can claim fulfillment in the sense that the United States has done its share in maintaining Western defenses while others were weak. It is now time for our partners to assume their share of the burden. Fourth, most of our allies have been negligent, failing to live up to their promises in terms of defense contributions. Fifth, the reasons for our temporary assumption of alliance leadership no longer exist, since many of our allies are now strong enough to defend themselves in every field except the nuclear one.

Finally, and most importantly, there is the argument of substitution or transformation. By placing greater reliance on indigenous conventional support, the United States can transform its present forward policy, which is losing credibility, into a stronger shared partnership that is indeed the kind of commitment that can "best be sustained over the long run."

EQUAL AMONG EQUALS

Risks inhere in any attempt to shift from a *primus inter pares* relationship with allies to the more modest role of *parus inter pares*. Retrenchment would not alter the fact that America's capabilities remain those of a superpower, and her quest for partnership must still be viewed in relative terms. If present force ratios and common defense contributions can be altered, partnership might then find new factual expression in regional arrangements that leave the major defense task (other than the strategic deterrent) in the adequate hands of local partners. If this is feasible in Southeast Asia, it should be no less applicable to the Eastern Mediterranean, an area of most interest to Western Europe, yet a place where American forces are the main element today. In 1947, the British decision to abandon its commitments to Greece and Turkey occurred in circumstances of impending national economic collapse. Was this transferral of responsibility by a European power to America something irrevocable and permanent? It now seems possible that Western Europe should resume a considerable role in Mediterranean defense; after all, the strategic implications of Soviet expansion into North Africa affect Europe directly and America only indirectly.

But hazards may attend specific American force reductions. If these were compensated by local build-ups on a step-by-step basis or accompanied by negotiated reductions of adversary strength, equilibrium would not be lost. Yet if United States reductions were interpreted as a prelude to abandonment or as signals of American unreliability, it is by no means certain that balance could be achieved. There would be no incentive for the adversary to bargain to obtain an agreed lower level of force, and allies might feel compelled to make an "agonizing reappraisal" of their alliance. An impending American withdrawal from Asia, for example, would provoke a major foreign-policy debate over Japan's defense and foreign-policy orientation, with profound implications for the stability of internal Japanese politics and for the peace of the entire region. In Western Europe, where the Soviet Union has in recent years been judged a "satisfied" power despite its greatly increased military capabilities, an American force reduction would not necessarily elicit a rise in European defense spending for self-help. Indeed, were American retrenchment publicly justified as a happy downward readjustment of force corresponding to new and improved conditions in the area, European incentives to take up the slack would be undermined. Inexorably, Europe might slide toward vulnerability and offer the Soviet Union a tempting chance to exploit suspicion of the "undependable," "neurotic" American ally.

Hamilton remarked in his first *Federalist* paper that when men are not able to decide important questions "from reflection and choice," they are "forever destined to depend . . . on accident and force. If there be any truth in the remark," he added, "the crisis at which we are arrived may with propriety be regarded as the era in which that decision is to be made; and a wrong election of the part we shall act may, in this view, deserve to be considered as the general misfortune of mankind."

The powerless take delight in the troubles of the powerful, which is why great powers are almost never liked and are respected only when their policies succeed. But even during times of trouble a great power can maintain respect and reputation by carefully changing the course of its policy. The change of course must seem reasonable, wise, internally consistent, and broadly supported at home. To institute such new policies will require strong bipartisan support of the kind which, until recently, undergirded the original set of American postwar commitments. To make the delicate adjustment to a less conspicuous new level of shared alliance commitments would demand a degree of domestic support that does not exist for current levels. The period of American withdrawal from Southeast Asia, a time of confusion and recrimination, could also become the occasion for a national resolve to assume steadier and more modest commitments in the future.

Machiavelli and de Tocqueville, two of America's tutors in world politics, had opposite views about the ability of a democracy to conduct foreign policy. The author of *The Prince* was optimistic about republics as reliable partners:

> . . . in such cases which involve imminent peril, there will be found somewhat more of stability in republics than in princes. For even if the republics were inspired by the same feelings and intentions as the princes, yet the fact of their movements being slower will make them take more time in forming resolutions, and therefore they will less promptly break their faith.

De Tocqueville, on the other hand, had fewer illusions:

> . . . a democracy is unable to regulate the details of an important undertaking, to persevere in a design, and to work out its execution in the presence of serious obstacles. It cannot combine its measures with secrecy, and it will not await their consequences with patience.

Before the Vietnam War, Machiavelli had the edge in the argument; now de Tocqueville surges ahead. The argument could continue indefinitely. Yet unhappy recent experience should give us new insights into the problem. Vietnam raises a serious question about the capacity of liberal democracy to engage in sustained "lonely" action in support of unilateral guarantees. Our traditional image of America—as a great, virtuous, and singular nation—was suited to the long Jeffersonian era of nonentanglement. The greatest domestic successes of American democracy were obtained with little or no outside help. But in more recent times our most effective action in international politics has invariably occurred only when the United States acted in close concert with many others.

If this is true, future American action abroad should be grounded in broad coalitions. This need for "multilateral legitimation" is not without risk. Yet the test of future American policy will be our success in encouraging indigenous coalitions to keep the peace and assure their own defense. As the United States reduces its military presence abroad and local strength grows, American forces and commanders ought to move out of the forefront and into the background of regional guarantee systems. Meanwhile, America's allies should heed with sympathy the current signs of our domestic difficulties. An unstable democratic *imperium* is not a good ally, but a reunified America, with a lower scale of commitments, could be a steady partner for the common problems that lie ahead.

REVIEW QUESTIONS

1. What are the various meanings of commitments?

2. How might United States foreign commitments be related to United States national resources?

3. How does the contemporary American alliance system differ from that system in the 1950s?

4. How compatible with each other are America's several regional alliance groupings?

5. How may attempts to obtain conditions of *détente* with Communist-bloc adversaries affect United States alliance relationships?

FOR FURTHER READING

Acheson, Dean: *Power and Diplomacy,* Harvard University Press, Cambridge, Mass., 1958.

Adler, Selig: *The Isolationist Impulse,* The Free Press, New York, 1966.

Almond, Gabriel: *The American People and Foreign Policy,* Praeger Publishers, Inc., New York, 1960.

Aron, Raymond: *Peace and War,* Doubleday Company, Inc., Garden City, N.Y., 1966.

Beard, Charles: *The Idea of National Interest,* The Macmillan Company, New York, 1934.

Brodie, Bernard: *Strategy in the Missile Age,* Princeton University Press, Princeton, N.J., 1959.

117

Brown, Seyom: *The Faces of Power,* Columbia University Press, New York, 1968.

Buchan, Alistair: *Problems of Modern Strategy,* Praeger Publishers, Inc., New York, 1970.

Cooper, Chester: *The Lost Crusade: America in Vietnam,* Dodd, Mead & Co., New York, 1970.

Corwin, Edward S.: *The President: Office and Powers, 1787-1957,* New York University Press, New York, 1957.

Feis, Herbert: *From Trust to Terror: The Onset of the Cold War, 1945-1950,* W.W. Norton & Company, Inc., New York, 1970.

————: *Between War and Peace: The Potsdam Conference,* Princeton University Press, Princeton, N.J., 1960.

Fulbright, J. William: *The Arrogance of Power,* Random House, Inc., New York, 1966.

Gilbert, Felix: *To the Farewell Address,* Princeton University Press, Princeton, N.J., 1961.

Gordon, Kermit: *Agenda for the Nation,* The Brookings Institution, Washington, D.C., 1968.

Graebner, Norman: *Ideas and Diplomacy: Readings in the Intellectual Tradition of American Foreign Policy,* Oxford University Press, New York, 1964.

Herzog, Arthur: *The War-Peace Establishment,* Harper & Row, Publishers, New York, 1964.

Hoffmann, Stanley: *Gulliver's Troubles,* McGraw-Hill Book Company, New York, 1968.

Howe, Irving: *The Dissenter's Guide to Foreign Policy,* Praeger Publishers, Inc., New York, 1968.

Huntington, Samuel P.: *The Common Defense,* Columbia University Press, New York, 1961.

Iklè, Fred Charles: *How Nations Negotiate,* Harper & Row, Publishers, New York, 1964.

Kissinger, Henry A.: *American Foreign Policy,* W.W. Norton & Company, Inc., New York, 1969.

Knorr, Klaus: *On the Uses of Military Power in the Nuclear Age,* Princeton University Press, Princeton, N.J., 1966.

Kohn, Hans: *American Nationalism: An Interpretive Essay,* The Macmillan Company, New York, 1957.

Kolko, Gabriel: *The Roots of American Foreign Policy,* Beacon Press, Boston, 1969.

Larson, David (ed.): *The "Cuban Crisis" of 1962,* Houghton Mifflin Company, Boston, 1963.

Lippmann, Walter: *Public Opinion,* Harcourt Brace Jovanovich, Inc., New York, 1922.

————: *U.S. Foreign Policy: Shield of the Republic,* Little, Brown and Company, Boston, 1943.

Liska, George: *Imperial America,* The Johns Hopkins Press, Baltimore, 1967.

Morgenthau, Hans: *In Defense of the National Interest,* Alfred A. Knopf, Inc., New York, 1951.

Niebuhr, Reinhold: *The Irony of American History,* Charles Scribner's Sons, New York, 1952.

Nixon, Richard M.: *U.S. Foreign Policy for the 1970's: A New Strategy for Peace,* The White House, Washington, D.C., 1970.

Osgood, Robert: *Alliances and American Foreign Policy,* The Johns Hopkins Press, Baltimore, 1968.

————: *Ideals and Self-interest in America's Foreign Relations,* University of Chicago Press, Chicago, 1953.

————and Robert Tucker, *Force, Order and Justice,* The Johns Hopkins Press, Baltimore, 1967.

Patterson, Thomas G. (ed.): *The Origins of the Cold War,* D.C. Heath & Company, Lexington, Mass., 1970.

Ransom, Harry Howe: *The Intelligence Establishment,* Harvard University Press, Cambridge, Mass., 1970.

Rosenau, James: *Public Opinion and Foreign Policy,* Random House, Inc., New York, 1961.

Schelling, Thomas: *Arms and Influence,* Yale University Press, New Haven, Conn., 1966.

Schwarz, Urs: *American Strategy: A New Perspective,* Doubleday & Company, Inc., Garden City, N.Y., 1966.

Seabury, Paul: *Power, Freedom and Diplomacy: The Foreign Policy of the United States,* Random House, Inc., New York, 1963.

———: *The Rise and Decline of the Cold War,* Basic Books, Inc., Publishers, New York, 1967.

Slater, Jerome: *Intervention and Negotiation,* Harper & Row, Publishers, New York, 1970.

Spanier, John: *Games Nations Play,* Praeger Publishers, Inc., New York, 1972.

Spykman, Nicholas: *America's Strategy in World Politics,* Harcourt Brace Jovanovich, Inc., New York, 1942.

Taylor, Maxwell: *Responsibility and Response,* Harper & Row, Publishers, New York, 1967.

Thompson, Sir Robert: *Revolutionary War in World Strategy, 1945–1969,* Taplinger Publishing Co., Inc., New York, 1970.

Tucker, Robert: *The Radical Left and American Foreign Policy,* The Johns Hopkins Press, Baltimore, 1971.

Ulam, Adam: *The Rivals: America and Russia Since World War II,* The Viking Press, Inc., New York, 1971.

Wilensky, Harold: *Organizational Intelligence,* Basic Books, Inc., Publishers, New York, 1967.

Williams, William Appleman: *The Tragedy of American Diplomacy,* Dell Publishing Co., Inc., New York, 1962.

Wolfers, Arnold: *Discord and Collaboration: Essays on International Politics,* Johns Hopkins Press, Baltimore, 1962.

INDEX